MW00767955

HEARING GOD IN A NOISY WORLD

Prayer as Listening

TIMOTHY L. OWINGS

Love to my dear friend, Ann Marie -

PEAKE ROAD
Macon, Georgia

Harriette

ISBN 1-57312-175-4

Hearing God in a Noisy World
Prayer as Listening

Timothy L. Owings

Smyth & Helwys Publishing, Inc.
6316 Peake Road
Macon, Georgia 31210-3960
1-800-747-3016

The paper used in this publication meets the minimum requirements of American National Standard for Information Sciences—Permanence of Paper for Printed Library Materials, ANSI Z39.48–1984.

Library of Congress Cataloging-in-Publication Data

Owings, Timothy.
Hearing God in a noisy world: prayer as listening/
Timothy L. Owings.
p. cm.
Includes bibliographical references.
ISBN 1-57312-175-4 (alk. paper)
1. Prayer—Christianity.
2. Listening—Religious aspects—Christianity.
I. Title.
BV10.2.095 1998
248.3'2—dc21 97-50020
CIP

CONTENTS

To my parents,
Neal and Eileen Owings,
and
Kathie's parents,
Charles and Betty Pignato,
Faithful hearers and doers of God's Word

FOREWORD

Timothy Owings has given to all of us a stirring and sustaining testimony of how faith in Christ can bolster us for the unforeseen, and often devastating, experiences of life. It is beyond question that we poor, besieged humans, buffeted so often by circumstances that seem cruel and inexplicable, need to learn from one another how to meet these "slings and arrows of outrageous fortune." This need to trade example and encouragement is infinitely enhanced when the light of Christ is thrown on our experience.

In this volume, Dr. Owings points us to the enduring strength found in the Scriptures. He reminds us that in and through the accounts of the Bible, God speaks to us, not nearly so judgmental as winsome and caring. Particularly helpful is his insistence that we respect the wholeness of the Bible and not see it as a collection of isolated snippets.

When the author turns to prayer, the reader is able to see a reflection of how this pastor-preacher has won his way through what might have been a shattering tragedy to a firm, bright confidence that all of the Lord's ways turn toward us with strength sufficient for the living of our days in confidence and in victory. One leaves the author's treatment of prayer greatly strengthened and humbly grateful that one who has passed through deep waters turns to the rest of us with the assurance that the promises of God are enough, more than enough, to get us safely to the farther shore.

—Gardner Taylor
Brooklyn, NY

ACKNOWLEDGMENTS

The writing of a book was a challenging and rewarding adventure. Like the living of a life, *Hearing God in a Noisy World,* has the mark of a personality expressed in the embrace of other personalities. I am indebted to so many who inspired me to write, encouraged me in the process of writing, and gave their unique gifts to me in the preparation of the manuscript.

At the very beginning my secretary, Mrs. Dede Maddox, carefully transcribed the five sermons that form the nucleus of the book. Her many labors of love for the staff and me and the members of the First Baptist Church of Augusta, Georgia, remind me often of her devoted love for God and God's people.

The ministerial staff and members of First Baptist Church continue to bless my life with their many words of encouragement for my preaching and their sharing of ministry with me. I especially thank Dr. Rodger B. Murchison, our church's associate pastor, for his support throughout this season of reflection, prayer, and writing. No pastor could ask for a more loving, supportive, or engaged community of faith than God has given me during my seven-plus years in Augusta. This community of faith is like no other I know of anywhere. I am indeed a blessed man.

Others have offered good gifts along the way. First Baptist Church members Mr. and Mrs. Robert Anderson's mountain home in Highlands, North Carolina, became the place where I first began to write. Thank you, Bobby and Jane, for loving my family and me and for giving us all the gift of retreat and family. Hearing the rushing water helped me listen. The academic and faith community of Oxford University's Regent's Park College were trusted friends during a sabbatical leave in June 1995. It was there the manuscript began to take on new life and vitality. I am especially indebted to Dr. John David Weaver and Dr. Paul Fiddes for their encouragement and insight during those days.

My new friends at Smyth & Helwys Publishing have guided me through the publication of this, my first book. A note both grateful and sad must be said about my literary agent, Mr. Ronald Haynes. Early in the prepublication process, Ron agreed to help me secure a publisher for this work. He read the manuscript, told me it was good work, and guided me in its final steps toward publication. Two weeks before the final manuscript was due, Ron suddenly passed away and entered life eternal. He was a faithful friend and colleague. I and many others shall miss him.

In closing, I have no words with which to express my gratitude to my wife, Kathie, and our three children, Nathan, Justin, and Lindsey. They have taught me so much about God, have shared with me so much of life, and have believed in me for so long, I cannot imagine life without them. Having such intimate and generous partners in life and faith is more than any man deserves. Thank you, precious family, for being God's listening hearts. I am grateful.

Introduction

THE LISTENING HEART

In a word, prayer is an ongoing but often interrupted conversation with God. Most of us first experience prayer in the embrace of parents, family, or a worshiping community. Truth is, we experience prayer before we consciously realize what prayer is all about. Prayers-not-our-own are overheard. We first eavesdrop on the prayers of parents, siblings, family friends, and others. We hear the words and are embraced by the experience. Early on we are curious listeners to all kinds of prayers, all the while not knowing what we're hearing. Even so, at first, our ignorance of prayer's meaning does not diminish the hearing of prayer's many words.

Not surprisingly, both the pious and the profane, and every degree of religious expression in between, know something of the experience of prayer. From infancy to adulthood, we first hear and then speak all kinds of prayers in times of distress, sorrow, confusion, gratitude, and uncertainty. With time, our vocabularies become crowded with prayer language. "A wing and a prayer," "She doesn't have a prayer," and "All you can do now is pray" are but a few common expressions using prayer language in response to everyday situations. Being "religious" has little to do with it. Human beings seem to know instinctively how central is this conversation with God we call prayer.

Reared in a religious home, I learned to pray simple prayers before meals and at bedtime. "God is great, God is good, let us thank Him for our food" and "Now I lay me down to sleep" were like shallow wading pools where I splashed cool water petitions before God. Both of these prayers, though associated with Christianity, are woven into the fabric of the American soul. *The New England Primer of 1781*, a standard children's textbook for generations, included "Now I lay me down to sleep" as part of the curriculum along with the ABCs.

For many, the praying of these prayers as children was like learning the Pledge of Allegiance to the Flag; it went along with growing up American. I remember a day when prayer began the public school day. Prior to 1964, I and millions of other American children recited the Lord's Prayer, were led in prayer by a teacher, or listened as a psalm was read from the Bible. Prayer and reciting the Pledge began the school day.

A couple of years ago the State of Georgia, where I make my home, instituted a daily "moment of silence" that some have concluded is a veiled way of reintroducing prayer into the daily public school routine. Though I'm not advocating a position on prayer in public schools, the point must be made: prayer has been and still is a meaningful, deeply personal behavior for most Americans. North and South, Jew and Gentile, believer and nonbeliever, and every ethnic color in the rainbow seem to find some place in their lives for prayer. So central is prayer to our common experience that we almost expect someone to pray at graduations, civic club meetings, weddings, and funerals. Only in the last thirty years has public prayer fallen on hard times. Though one would be hard-pressed to document a direct relationship between the increasing violence-fear-immorality syndrome in America and the demise of public prayer, many ask: Are these issues related to one another?

The Gallup organization routinely surveys tens of thousands of Americans on everything from crime to Christmas. Year after year an overwhelming majority of Americans say prayer is a part of their lives to some degree.[1] Among those surveyed in 1992–1993, what seemed to matter most was not the degree of religious devotion or involvement in some faith community, but rather the simple affirmation "Yes, I pray."

Books on how to pray, what to pray, when to pray, and why we pray are legion. In this century significant works on prayer would include George Buttrick's *Prayer*, Harry Emerson Fosdick's *The Meaning of Prayer*, Thomas Merton's *Contemplative Prayer*, Richard Foster's *Prayer: Finding the Heart's True Home*, and many others. Without exception, these well-written and thoughtful books speak of prayer as dialogue. Yet the dialogue they enjoin stresses almost exclusively the human side of the conversation. To be sure, my understanding of prayer has grown, and my awareness of the multifaceted wonder of prayer has widened because of their contributions.

Even so, I continue to ask questions: What is God saying? How is God responding to my prayers? What do I do with the answers I sense come from God who is, I trust, responding to my prayers? My questions have grown to the point where I'm wondering if others feel the same way. Conduct your own survey. Ask a friend: Does God answer your prayers? With few exceptions, my hunch is that thoughtful people will respond by saying something like, "Of course. Why would I pray to a God who doesn't answer my prayers?" I agree!

When we pray, we use language-words-thoughts to commune with God. Communion, however, suggests a two-sided, two-way dialogue. If prayer is conversation with God, I must ask: How does God commune with me? What venue, what means, and what part of me receives and interprets God's communication? How do I distinguish God's voice from my own feelings? How do I hear God's voice in this noisy world?

For as long as human beings have recorded their thoughts, the *heart* has been the place, the space, the human sanctuary where God has addressed us. The heart, used in this way, does not refer to the body's physical, blood-pumping organ. Rather, the heart is the unseen, spiritual vitality-reality resident in us all affecting our entire life physically, emotionally, and spiritually. Like the microprocessor in a computer, the heart sorts out all the data flowing in and out of one's inner self. The heart decides whether a remark is kind or mean. The heart takes in a lush meadow of wildflowers and interprets such beauty as the handiwork of God. The heart tells our tear ducts to let their briny tide flow when a meaningful relationship has ended. In more ways than we can consciously imagine, the heart controls much of who we are and how we function in relationship to God, ourselves, and others.

Quite simply, we could not be the laughing, singing, weeping, feeling creation we are without our spiritual heart. Just as the microchip enables a box of resistors, wires, and boards to be called a computer, so the heart enables us to be called human. Greater than God's creative gifts of sensing eyes, ears, touch, taste, and smell, more miraculous than the power of the mind, the heart is the place where we speak with God and where God speaks with us.

So has it always been. In the early days of 1995, I had the opportunity of visiting in the Middle East. For two days the group I was leading immersed ourselves in the treasures and awesome glory of ancient Egypt. That civilization, towering over the Fertile Crescent for more than 2,000 years, had a deep-rooted belief in the afterlife. The whole ritual process of embalming a body and filling the tomb with treasures was an attempt by the ancient Egyptians to empower one's continued existence in the life beyond this life.

Central to that belief was the role of the heart in determining one's future state. One of the more intriguing scenes from the tombs of the Pharaohs is called "the weighing of the heart." After death, the deceased was brought before the god Osiris by the god of death, Anubis. At that moment the person's heart was weighed in the scales opposite a feather. If the scales tipped in favor of the heart, the person was declared wicked, and the heart was eaten by a waiting jackal. On the other hand, if the heart was lighter than the feather, the person was pronounced righteous. The ancient Egyptians believed one's eternal destiny was determined by the condition of the heart. Rather than being a ruthless civilization as some have suggested, the ancient Egyptians valued and encouraged ethical and moral living. They believed the heart was the place where one's earthly life found direction and where one's soul would, in the afterlife, find vindication.

Today we still speak of the heart as the soul-center of life. A person who lives passionately is said to have "heart." To put one's whole heart into something is to give it one's all. The last stanza to the beloved gospel song "Wherever He Leads, I'll Go" begins with these words: "My heart, my life, my all I bring to Christ who loves me so." To give God one's heart is to give God one's life and one's all. To live from the heart is to live deeply, fully, passionately. Whatever else prayer may be, at its core, prayer must be speaking to and listening for God from the heart.

All the enduring works on prayer have given good counsel on the speaking heart. In the pages that follow I invite you to explore with me the other side of prayer I call the listening heart. Like the dialogue of prayer itself, our journey into prayer will be conversational. For my part, I embark on an autobiographical journey through four and a half decades of living. Through real pain, experienced early in my life through circumstances not of my choosing, I learned to listen for the persistent, loving voice of God. My story, though uniquely mine, may have stops along the way similar to yours.

Frederick Buechner reminds us that "all theology, like all fiction, is at its heart autobiography."[2] I have learned how true this profoundly simple analogy is. The impressions-leadings-feelings of my heart I have discerned as the voice of God are distinctively different from all other feelings in my life. At times puzzling and always challenging and hard-to-define, God's voice has whispered its wonder through the many marvelous and maddening experiences of my forty-four years. There is, in my judgment, no other way for the Holy One to address us personally. God speaks to us, if God speaks at all, in our individuality and our history. Such is the mystery and invitation to pray and to listen and to commune with God.

So the journey begins. The first half of our journey asks, How do we tune our hearts to hear God's voice? In four chapters we will explore the ways God speaks through creation, the Bible, the faith community, and prayer. The second half of our journey asks: What are God's answers to prayer, and how do we respond to them? I believe God answers prayer. Still the questions linger: What are God's answers, and what might they mean? As we come to God with a listening heart, we can grow in our love for God and begin to celebrate God's voice and God's presence in our lives more fully.

To these questions and others we'll meet along the way, we now turn. As we make this journey together, I hope we will discover the listening heart to be the place where we meet God and discover to our delight and continued fascination God's voice.

Notes

[1]The following sentence begins the Gallup report on prayer: "Nearly nine adults in ten in the United States say they pray to God at least occasionally." Robert Bezilla, ed., *Religion in America: 1992–1993* (Princeton: The Princeton Religion Research Center, 1994) 49.

[2]Frederick Buechner, *The Sacred Journey* (San Francisco: Harper Collins, 1982) 1.

Chapter 1

SPEAK TO MY HEART

The listening heart, though created to hear and speak and commune with God, does not find its true purpose apart from personal experience. The Bible is clear on this one indisputable fact: God addressed every person we meet in Scripture through their own life experience and history. As best I can determine, every person in the Bible experienced God with their feet firmly on earth. Persons we call "saints" were human beings like us whose lives were addressed and saved and graced by God in the midst of their daily lives. So it is with us.

In this chapter I relive a life-changing experience in my early years that even now affects my life in profound ways. Through this moment in my story, you may find yourself relating to similar moments where God spoke and continues to speak through the events you have lived. In the second half of the chapter, I explore how a common tuning fork pictures God's invitation to hear God's voice in this noisy world.

An Unwanted Visitor

June 1954 was a tragic and confusing month in my life and for my family. I was thirteen months old, the third of four children born to Neal and Eileen Owings. Living in the Miami, Florida, suburb of Hialeah, as the summer days grew warmer and the humidity rose, parents throughout the nation, and especially in the humid South, were keenly aware of the threat of poliomyelitis. Still two years away, a polio vaccine was nonexistent. To lessen the possibility of infection, parents were advised to keep their children away from public swimming pools and theaters. The prevailing wisdom of the day believed children were more likely to contract the dreaded virus in public places.

Because I was still an infant, my mother scrupulously guarded my contacts with other children. On the other hand, my ten-year-old sister, Jan, and eight-year-old brother, Neal, went regularly to the pool and the movies. My only contact with other children was in the nursery of our church. Little did we know how odd and impossible-to-understand would be the changes in all our lives as we lived through that first summer month of 1954.

Jan was the first to notice a change in my behavior. Ordinarily a happy baby—my mother told me not long ago I never met a person I didn't like—I suddenly became irritable and sullen. Feeling warm, Mom took my temperature, called the doctor, and soon I was taken from his office to Variety Children's Hospital in south Miami. A spinal tap was performed, and the dreaded word "polio" tumbled out of the doctor's mouth.

Gratefully, I don't remember any of this. Even so, this one event early in my life had a shaping-transforming quality about it that affected my family and me in profound and life-changing ways. Mom has since told me the only time she ever saw my father weep was that day of days they left me at the hospital. As she tells the story, Dad came home, threw himself on the bed, and wept, asking why God had cursed him so. At that moment, for my parents, my family, and yes, even for me—unaware of what was happening in my infant life–heaven was silent. Today Dad would be the first to tell you—I know this sounds crazy to some—polio turned out to be a positive turning point in all our lives, lives that are still moving around the greater purposes of God. Anyone who has endured a traumatic personal or family health crisis knows how such experiences alter forever the landscape of one's personal and relational life. Though wounded, the listening heart refuses to turn a deaf ear to all that has happened and is happening around it. Listen we must, even if dissonance is all we hear.

After a number of days in the hospital, polio had worked its madness on my left leg. During those years tens of thousands of children, teenagers, and adults endured the onslaught of polio. More than a few died. Others were left with withered arms, two withered legs, or a painful combination of afflicted arms and legs. One of my earliest memories of visiting Variety Children's Hospital as a three-year-old is that of seeing a ward full of iron lungs, some with tiny heads poking out. Polio was the plague of the 1940s and 1950s. Many still feel the aftershocks of polio in what is now being called "post-polio syndrome."

Anyone who has been there, or someplace like "there," knows how impossible it is to walk away from a crippling physical illness such as polio without a limp. Honestly–not for pity's sake–the limp distorts not only one's walk, but the landscape and people and events one sees as one walks. All of life from that point on has a jostled, dipping, and twisted quality about it. With every step the horizon dips a bit, the trees move first to the left, then to right. Hippity-hoppity, with a staccato stridency, the sidewalk is a bit further away for my left leg than my right. Weight is forever shifted to my "strong" side. The aftershock of a polio-like insult lasts a lifetime. I would later discover and know with every step how real and obvious, and at times physically and emotionally painful, such a limp can be.

I survived hospitalization and came home. Dad bought iron pipes and constructed an exercise walk much like the one used at the hospital. A brace, attached to high-top Edwards orthopedic shoes, was soon fitted to my left leg and attached around my waist like a noose. Having taken my first steps only weeks prior to polio's visit, I had to learn to walk all over again. This time, walking meant having a heavy brace around my leg as I squeezed the parallel pipes to steady my every step. Overnight, polio and its residual aftershocks had become an unwanted but permanent part of my life. What would I do? How would I, a fourteen-month newcomer to life, handle these traumatic changes? How would my parents and siblings, family and church, neighbors, doctors, therapists, and all who knew me and loved me respond?

Through this entire experience my parents' faith in God and the faithful prayers of God's people became wells of hope and strength. God was working in all our lives to bring about God's greater purposes. The only way polio could become what Dad first called a curse would be if first my parents and, later, I allowed that definition of polio to prevail. My parents made a wise choice. They decided the word "curse" would never describe polio's presence in my life.

Words more redemptive, more purposeful were there waiting to be heard. Mom and Dad's listening hearts heard those words and passed them on to me. So much of what I have learned about prayer still resonates with redemptive words such as hope, optimism, courage, and faith.

Reflecting back on those early years, dependent as I was on my parents, Jan, Neal, and later my younger sister Beth, a church family, and wonderful family friends, God was working through the experience of polio and a kaleidoscope of other everyday experiences. God's work, God's voice, God's presence, was and still is beaming a love and strength to my life I perhaps would not have known had polio not been such a significant detour in some preplanned life itinerary.

Fortunately, I came through polio with minimal physical consequences. Yes, I walk with a discernible limp. Yes, doctors have told me I will probably spend the latter years of my life with some degree of pain. Yes, there are activities I've not been able to enjoy (only water skiing and track come to mind). But at every turn, with every step, I was taught and have come to know firsthand that God is present and empowering my life through the experience of prayer.

So I ask: What is the context in which meaningful prayer occurs? How do we tune our hearts to recognize, hear, and enjoy the voice of God? These are important and foundational questions. The fact is, we can't take another step–even with braces–until we first learn to recognize the voice of God above the other voices blasting their message our way. According to the Bible, the heart is the receptive dimension of our beings through which God speaks. How do we tune the heart to hear God's winsome voice?

Strike the Tuning Fork

Musicians know the answer. The tuning fork, more specifically the 440 tuning fork, is the standard by which all concert instruments are tuned. Granted, tuning forks come in many sizes. The universally recognized tuning fork for musicians, however, is designed to vibrate at 440 cycles per second. The sound it makes is concert "A." With a 440 tuning fork, you can tune almost any instrument in the world.

For example, a piano tuner will strike the 440 tuning fork, place it on the grand piano, and from this one sound, tune all the strings, all 88 keys of the piano. A 440 tuning fork can tune a violin, a trumpet, an oboe, a clarinet, and scores of other instruments. 440 is the standard. There is no other.

Does God have a standard by which we tune our lives to recognize and hear God's voice? How do we know as we meander through life whether or not God is speaking to us, or perhaps the voice we are hearing is not God's voice at all? Perhaps we may think we're hearing the voice of God but, actually, the voice we're hearing is not God. Rather, we're hearing our own lust, our own ego, our own whims disguised as God-talk. Confusions abound, and many are confused.

At the dawn of the Christian movement, John the Baptist, the herald who announced the coming of the Messiah, was one of the confused listeners to God's voice. From his mother's womb, God had called John to proclaim the coming of Jesus (Luke 1:11-17). The years passed. Both John and Jesus matured into young adulthood. John headed for the desert to thunder the judgment and coming of God. Jesus, apprenticed to Joseph in the carpenter's trade, would soon leave his chisels and mallets for the harsh Jordan valley, a water baptism, a lonely desert, a cross, and a borrowed tomb.

The time came for these two towering personalities to meet each other on the stage of history. God had struck the eternal tuning fork and placed it on Jesus of Nazareth. His life was resonating the sounds of God. Through Jesus' personality, his mind, his voice, his heart, God's voice was beginning to bounce in all directions. According to the Fourth Gospel, John saw Jesus coming toward him in the desert and blurted out, "Here is the Lamb of God who takes away the sin of the world" (John 1:29). Some of John's disciples left him and followed Jesus.

Now, months later, Jesus' ministry was off and running in a whirlwind of activity. Healings, feedings, preaching, and controversy filled his every day. At the same time the burly voice of the Baptist was silenced. The voice that once trumpeted the coming "Lamb of

God" was now a prison-bound whimper. Herod Antipas had arrested John and thrown him in prison. Soon John's head would lie in a pool of blood, delivered to a young woman on a silver platter. For now, John lay rotting in Herod's dungeon while Jesus drew thousands to hear his every word. John was confused. Wouldn't you have been? John's questions are so obvious and make so much sense. Was Jesus the Son of God? Was he the Messiah? Was he the "Lamb of God?" Or did John miss it?

In confusion and, no doubt, great anguish, John sent word to Jesus. Listen to the account as Matthew told it. "When John heard in prison what the Messiah was doing, he sent word by his disciples and said to him, 'Are you the one who is to come, or are we to wait for another?' " (11:2-3). When Jesus heard John's question, he sent John's disciples back with a profound but curious answer. The blind were seeing, the deaf were hearing, the lame were walking, the dead were being raised, and the poor were hearing good news. Then, after Jesus sent John's messengers away, he turned to the crowd and talked about his imprisoned friend. With near ironic similarity, the crowd listening to Jesus didn't understand his message any better than they had understood John's. Jesus was as confusing to them as he often is to us. Hear what Jesus said to the people.

> But to what can I compare this generation? It is like children sitting in the marketplaces and calling to one another, "We played the flute for you, and you did not dance; we wailed, and you did not mourn." For John came neither eating nor drinking, and you say, "He has a demon" [meaning, "he's crazy"]; the Son of Man came eating and drinking, and they say, "Look, a glutton and a drunkard, a friend of tax collectors and sinners!" (11:16-19a)

What is Jesus saying? I think I hear him say, if we are not careful, if we are not listening for God's voice, we too can act like spoiled children playing games; wanting God to dance to our tune, rather than letting our lives be tuned to God. If we are not careful, we will tune our lives to the uncertain sounds close to 440, but so slightly dissonant. Tradition, uncritically embraced, can vibrate at

430 cycles per second. New Age sounds can shimmer at 450 cycles per second. The former, flat with lifeless sameness; the latter, sharp with avant-garde flair. God-like sounds—so very close to God's voice—but not God. Distinct sounds, vibrating with noisy regularity close to God's 440, but so distant and dissonant. Such auditory confusion is no stranger to anyone with a listening heart.

What is worse, if we are not careful, we may miss hearing the voice of God altogether. We will confuse books about prayer and prayer meetings and prayer groups—all of which can be deeply satisfying—with intimate time alone with God. How easy it is to miss or, having heard, "miss-understand" the voice of God. We can so easily confuse worship services accompanied by wonderful orchestras, trained choirs, thoughtful preaching, and sixty-minute timed order with authentic, life-changing, God-encountering worship. To be sure, empowering, deeply moving, God-encountering worship is enriched by music, preaching, and liturgy, but it must never be eclipsed by these important elements of worship. God-encountering worship may be experienced while we are surrounded by hundreds of other people, but it is always a one-on-one, heart-to-heart communion with God.

The Christian community today is "wowed" and can even be misled by the mega-church, television-bright lights-camera angle atmosphere so prevalent in larger churches. I speak as one who knows. Each week my church's Sunday morning service is broadcast to thousands of homes in our part of Georgia and in South Carolina. If we are not careful—as a pastor, if *I* am not careful—we'll settle for worship as performance rather than worship as relationship and reunion with God.

In the routine daily-ness of our lives, even without our conscious consent, we can and often do become so attuned to earth sounds—wars and rumors of wars, death and disease, abandonments and abusings, promotions and stock-splits—that we miss the simple note struck by God in Jesus when he said, "My kingdom is not from this world" (John 18:36).

In Jesus, God's kingdom is not manufactured by this world, created by this world, endorsed by this world, or established and maintained by this world. God's kingdom strikes a distinctive, radical, "other" note. That sound is the eternal heartbeat of God to which we are invited to tune our hearts and, in so doing, find the rapturous reunion and relationship God created us to have with Him.

A story from my more recent history best illustrates this dynamic reality. Bill Curry, former head football coach at the University of Kentucky, is an exceptional human being. His Christian commitment is perhaps best illustrated by his great gift in motivating young people. To say "Bill Curry" is to speak of integrity, character, and class. Through the mysterious and wonderful providence of God, Bill and I became close friends during the three seasons he coached at Alabama. The Alabama football family is full of many wonderful people who love the game and love young people. Unfortunately, as is true in so many organizations, the shouting minority of nay-sayers can poison what is best for the many. Such was the case during the Curry years at Alabama. Through it all, I never heard my friend say in public, or in the many times we met in private, one negative remark about Alabama, his opponents within the program and the larger Alabama "family," or the circumstances surrounding his leaving. Bill Curry is one person through whom I have heard the voice of God. I've often found his heart beating with God's 440.

During those brief years, Bill gave me a pass to attend football practice. Not all that big a deal, the athletic department at Alabama would give boosters, alumni, and friends of the University passes to practice. Nobody, however, had a pass like mine. Bill had personally given me a pass and put a note on the back. At times—such as before the Tennessee or Auburn games—Alabama practices were closed (not that anybody would want to know what they were doing!). Even so, I had a pass that allowed me access to those closed practices. Bill wrote on the back of my pass these words: "Let this preacher in to any practice for religious reasons."

You may think that's quite an honor—and it was—that the coach and team needed the encouragement and support of a Baptist preacher. But don't confuse glamour with fact. The only reason I could get into those practices was simple: Bill Curry knew and still knows I'm stupid when it comes to understanding and analyzing football. X's and O's are as strange to me as Greek would be to an offensive tackle. Auburn could kidnap me, torture me, lay me out on a rack, and say "Give us the Alabama plays," and I wouldn't know what I'd seen or what they were doing. Knowing that, Bill let me come out there and watch the guys practice.

I'll always remember the time I walked out on the artificial surface of the practice field during a full pads, rough-and-tumble scrimmage before that year's game with arch rival Tennessee, played in Knoxville. The closer I got to the line of scrimmage, the louder and painfully deafening was this awful sound coming from two huge speakers positioned on the field. I finally figured out the speakers were blasting crowd noise toward the players on the field.

Get this. Somebody on the football staff had recorded crowd noise from an actual game and amplified it. This shouting, dissonant, piped-in-noise blasted the team practicing on the field like mortars shelling enemy positions. I walked up to Bill, cupped my hands, and shouted, "Why are you doing that?" He smiled, cupped his hands, and rifled my ears with "What did you say?" The funnies aside, he asked, "Have you ever been on the field at Nyland Stadium during a football game?" I said, "No." "When we play there Saturday, we've got to be able to cope with this kind of noise, only worse."

Then it hit me. As the quarterback got under center and called the signals, the guards, tackles, ends, and backs had to be able to hear the sound of their quarterback calling the play over the raucous noise of the crowd. If they couldn't tune their ears to hear their quarterback above the noise of the crowd, they couldn't run their plays and stay in the game.

In that moment God gave me an insight into the relationship God wants to have with us. God struck His tuning fork. I sensed God say to me, "This is how it is with you, Tim. Learn to tune out the cacophony of crowd noise around you so you can tune your heart to my voice. Learn to listen for me."

From that pivotal moment in June 1954, when polio did its thing in my body, to this moment in my life, I've been seeking ways—sometimes successful, sometimes not—to do just that. Whatever journey you're taking, I have a hunch you're trying to listen to the same winsome, nurturing voice of God. In the next four chapters I suggest four ways God tunes our hearts to Him. Through my own life experience and uniquely in the journey with polio God has spoken and continues to speak. So it is in your journey with God. Every life experience, every turn in the road, every "gee-whiz" moment, every heart-rending tragedy can be an opportunity to hear God's voice above the noise of the moment. To that adventure we now turn.

Chapter 2

THIS IS MY FATHER'S WORLD

I learned a hymn in childhood that still reminds me "this is my Father's world." Is it? What, with so much seeming terror loose in nature, so many diseases, viruses, cancers, and crippling-maiming-tragic accidents stalking our humanity, so unrelenting an attack on the environment by insensitive and greedy individuals and corporations, can we believe this planet is still God's world? With the Holocaust still haunting this century's memory, with the continuing struggle of the world's oppressed for justice, with child abuse and abandonments of all kinds at epidemic proportions, can we still say this is God's world?

Some would say the world has never been God's. Whether said or unsaid, many live as if God is absent, sick, or worse, dead. Others might concede a time when humanity was more innocent, more rooted in the warm earth, when God was a partner in tilling the garden of creation. Still others insist—some say naively—the hymn is right. This was, is, and will always be God's world. Because God created all that is, God, by right, has first claim on that which God created.

I'm one of those in the last camp. No, I'm not naive. I'm fully aware that many of earth's forests are being raped and its oceans poisoned, plains destroyed, and valleys trashed. Like you, I witness the destruction of a tornado, a hurricane, an epidemic, a famine, and ask, Is this God's world? Much of the evidence suggests God has abandoned the world God created. I have had my own reasons to agree.

Polio taught me early on a deep respect for the basic laws of physics. Gravity works. A leg that has little muscle tone and fewer-than-normal working nerve endings will not do certain things, no matter how much your mind says otherwise. The Buddhists are wrong on this one. Pain is not an illusion. One cannot, in an absolute sense, will to be healed.

Exceptions abound. Like you, I've known extraordinary persons who have held back the marching tide of malignancy through sheer willpower, optimism, and courage. Three and a half years have passed since her death. Naomi "Nopi" Barnard lingers in my gallery of heroes. Diagnosed with cancer in the early 1980s, she refused to give up and bounced back from countless brushes with death. Through it all Nopi lived a courageous, giving, generous life until she died on February 2, 1994. Nopi's husband was our representative in Congress for sixteen years. Now retired, Doug Barnard is a public servant in the finest sense of the word. His faith informed and guided the many decisions he made as a member of Congress. Election after election, the people of Georgia's tenth district made their choice: they wanted Congressman Barnard to represent them and be their voice in Washington.

Doug, in a moment of lighthearted candor, once defined Washington as "ten square miles surrounded by reality." Closer to home, Doug's precious Nopi was a remarkable Christian lady surrounded by a reality she refused to let control her life. Yes, she had cancer. But Nopi refused to let cancer have her.

We live in a world where cancers show up in the most unlikely and always unwanted places. I've not known a person who honestly thanked God for cancer. Only a person whose mind was malignant would voice such a prayer. Even so, to enjoy the gift of life is to know the risks of living. With life's laughter come life's tears. So it is for all of us at every turn in the journey. And when the journey gets difficult, when the mountains once beautiful crash around us, when the seas once placid roar with a vengeance, we rightfully ask: What kind of reality surrounds us? If God is speaking to us through creation, what kind of God is this One with whom we have to do?

Our options are basically two: (1) We can believe the reality around us is malignant and evil; or (2) we can believe the risky and outrageous notion that creation belongs to God, and that as God's domain, creation is the arena-place-environment in which we meet our true selves in fellowship with the God who made us. I choose the latter. This is God's world, created by God's power and sustained within God's purposes. The first choice throws my life into a mindless, fatalistic fog. In such a place the reality surrounding me is opaque, menacing, confusing, and indifferent. Coping is mere groping, feeling my way through an ever-thickening fog that never lifts. True, the fog may roll in, but none of us has to live as if the fog is all there is all the time.

The second choice—at once both risky and even outrageous—believes the reality in which we live and move and have our being is God. Fashioned by God's creative genius, the world is neither menacing nor kind. Rather, the world-universe-cosmos is the space, the environment in which we experience reality. The Bible calls this reality creation. By faith, I believe the reality in which I find myself is not an indifferent fog, but rather a magnificent mystery. Holding this mystery, this creation-reality together, is nothing less than a God-designed tension between chaos and order.[1] To our surprise, this chaos-order tension is the very stability that keeps the world balanced and functioning.

In his superb book *In the Beginning God*, Dr. John Weaver surveys the current research being done by physicists, mathematicians, and cosmologists. Of the many intriguing discoveries being made by science today, Dr. Weaver draws our attention to the tension inherent within creation between greater entropy within the universe and great complexity within life. That is, the universe is moving inexorably toward either "Heat Death" or "The Big Crunch." This entropy—call it chaos in the making—is a fact of the physical universe. On the other hand, life seems to move in the direction of greater complexity and order. The continuing growth of the collective human intellect alone is but one example of this phenomenon. Weaver writes, "While entropy increases in the universe system as a whole, complex life-forms develop in a manner that seems to run counter to the pattern by taking in energy in a low entropy form and discarding it in a high entropy form." Add to this cosmic irony the fact that "the universe is as it is because if it were different, we would not be here to observe it," and you have what scientists call "The Anthropic Principle" by which we understand purpose and design in all creation.[2]

If you're like me, a simple illustration would help us bring this amazing reality into focus. Do you remember playing on the teeter-totter? Remember how challenging it was to find another child who was just about your size to take the other side of the board? If you could find the right partner, the two of you would laugh and hiccup high and low on that simple playground toy till your legs gave out. On the other hand, if you were overweight—as I always was—and the choices for partners were, shall I say, lighter, try as you might, the fun couldn't begin.

Like that playground toy, God has placed on the great balance of creation chaos and order (greater entropy and greater complexity bound together by the Anthropic Principle). They are remarkably balanced in God's creative genius. At times chaos seems to triumph; at other times order is the wonder of our lives.

For example, the laws of physics at work within creation, and thus God-designed, have a remarkable predictability about them. Given the right atmospheric pressure, temperature, humidity, and prevailing winds, you'll find yourself in the midst of a thunderstorm. Water flows downhill (aren't you glad?!), leaves turn colors in the fall, flowers bloom in the spring, weeds pepper your yard in places you can't get grass to grow, children grow up, babies are born, living beings of all sizes and complexities die.

In confusing moments, when the blizzard hits or the tornado touches down, we say, "Creation has gone mad." Has it? In the early weeks of 1995, an earthquake rocked and rolled Japan with disastrous consequences. The death toll climbed into the thousands; property damage was extensive. What happened? The unstable plates of the earth moved, the ground trembled, freeways and houses built above earth's shifting crust fell, people perished, and property was destroyed.

Forgive me if this sounds heartless and insensitive to human suffering in all its diversity, but creation is not broken. To the contrary, God's creation is acting within the laws governing its very existence. Would we want it otherwise? Would we really want God to suspend the laws of nature because we, at a particular moment, didn't like them? I think not. The world that can delight us is also the world that can—and sometimes does—destroy us.

For the occasional times when nature's chaos disrupts our planned futures, there are innumerable—and often unnoticed—times when God's creation goes about its orderly business to our benefit—and without our conscious awareness. The sun shines day after day, the rains come and irrigate the earth, vegetables appear in our grocery stores, apple trees laden with fall's bounty dot a mountainside, and waves gently lap the seashore where we've come to spend a week's vacation. With unconfessed pleasure, we enjoy and even glory in daily order. Chaos, however, in a brief few moments, can forever alter our future and put a detour on the leisurely highway of life we're traveling.

Secular writers, as well as theologians, are reminding us of this "chaos-order" phenomenon within creation. A front-page article that appeared in the *Wall Street Journal* summarizes the work of environmental historian Donald Worster.[3] In his judgment, contrary to the prevailing thought of hundreds of years, creation is not moving toward greater sophistication and order. *Wall Street* writer Dennis Farney said, "Nature, once viewed as inherently orderly, is coming to be viewed by many (although certainly not all) scientists as inherently disorderly." Creation, left to itself, reasons Dr. Worster, seems to favor a tension between weeds and grass, thorns and flowers, cancer and health, thunderstorms and gentle rains. The word is balance.

This balance is central to the reality expressed long ago in the Bible. God fashioned a predictable creation that is both vividly harmonious and at times frighteningly hostile. Today scientists have embraced the word "design" and yes, even purpose in describing the reality of the universe.[4] Within the magnificent complexity of creation is this observable tension between chaos (entropy) and order (sophistication). The Psalmist used poetry in the long ago describing what science is now "discovering" when he said, "The heavens are telling the glory of God; and the firmament proclaims his handiwork" (Ps 19:1).

Sadly, some conservative Christians have so separated the theologies of creation and salvation that environmental and social concerns have been considered the agenda of liberals. Though unsaid, conservatives have advocated *de facto* a "chaos" mentality toward creation believing the world is soon coming to an end. "Why bother with trying to reclaim the rain forests or clean up the environment," they reason, "if Jesus is coming again in this generation?" Such reasoning theologically divorces humankind's responsibility under God for creation from creation's endtime goal of "a new heaven and a new earth." Unwittingly, believers can subscribe to a kind of "chaos" cosmology, locating God's work and presence only in the human heart's response to Christ. I object.

For the first time since the seventeenth century, scientists are beginning to admit there is a point beyond which they cannot go in understanding reality. That point is the hard-to-put-in-a-petri-dish reality called "purpose." The picture of creation revealed in the Bible is not one of disorder, but rather a dynamic and resplendent balance between order and chaos. Our experience tells us this is so. Could this unpredictable equilibrium between order and chaos be God's gift summoning us to greater sensitivity to our environment and great responsibility for our choices? In my judgment, an awesome opportunity is staring us in the face. In terms of our journey into prayer, what role does the listening heart play in hearing God's voice through creation's mixed bag? When faced with creation's teeter-totter reality, how do we listen for God's voice? We must choose.

So it was and still is for me in my collision with polio's chaos. Sinister virus and crippler that it was, polio predictably ran its course in my body. Its orderly progression from fever to braces to limp wreaked havoc with my body (chaos) all the while following a predictable pattern (order). Its effects? A withered left leg, temporary and perhaps some yet unknown heartbreak, and—most important for the listening heart—a questioning and searching mind have been polio's residual effects. At times I've been tempted to refer to myself as a "victim" of polio, but the word has never been spoken to me, nor has it ever passed my lips. Victims are to be pitied as helpless to address their circumstances.

I am no victim. I am the recipient of a virus and its aftereffects. All those gifts and ten thousand, thousand more bear their witness to the predictability of God's orderly-chaotic creation. Yes, I have a limp, but I refuse to let the limp have me. What about you? Could it be that God has surrounded your ten square miles of life with a greater reality through which God is speaking to you? Could God's orderly-chaotic creation be beaming messages to you about what is really important in life and what will endure long after you have left the stage of history?

Perhaps a story will open a window on this idea. Though not athletic, I have always lived a vigorous, active life. As I began the seventh grade, I asked my Dad if we could build a sailboat. God gave my Dad a gift when, as a teenager, his stepfather taught him how to make things with wood. Before I came along, Dad built our family's first house from the ground up: foundation, plumbing, carpentry, masonry, electrical work, roof, everything.

Later, in the early 1950s, when I was an infant, Dad built a ski boat. Sold years earlier, I remember it only from pictures. At age twelve, with stories told and retold of Dad's boat-building prowess (you'd have to know my Dad to know how much he enjoys retelling a story you've heard a dozen times), I longed to sail. Living close to the water, something fascinated me about sailboats. Shock of all shocks, Dad said, "We'll build it." We ordered the plans, studied them for a couple of months, and decided it was time to get busy building our boat. The boat we chose to build was the Snipe, a sleek fifteen-and-a-half-foot one-design sloop.

I'll never forget the Saturday we started to build the Snipe. Even more memorable was the day we launched the boat appropriately christened *Hours*. After eight months of Dad's blood and sweat and my tears, our pride and joy slipped off the trailer into the waiting arms of Biscayne Bay. You would have had to have been there to fully appreciate this moment. The boat actually floated and looked beautiful bobbing there in the water.

Only one problem: neither Dad nor I knew how to sail. Mind you, we'd had a couple of lessons in another boat, but neither one of us had ever sailed a Snipe. We stood on the pier for a few minutes, admiring our work, when Dad said, "Let's rig her up and take her for her maiden voyage." Sounded good to me. Dad stepped on the front deck of the boat and, before you could say "splash," the boat dipped to port and swung to starboard and dumped my Dad in the Bay. Sloshing his way up the boat ramp, soaked from his head to his deck shoes, Dad walked out on the pier a second time and said, "Let me try that again." He did, and the boat summarily threw him in the Bay a second time. Forgive me, but my mom, my sister, a friend, and I were holding our sides laughing. Had "America's Funniest Home Videos" been around at the time, we would have won the grand prize.

Here came Dad a second time, sloshing his way up the boat ramp, soaked from top to bottom, scratching his head trying to figure out why the boat was so unstable. Then it hit us. Almost simultaneously, we looked at each other and said, "The centerboard!" We forgot to insert the heavy aluminum centerboard into the boat. Retrieving the centerboard from the trailer, we slipped it into the boat, rigged her up, and proudly sailed her across a gentle Biscayne Bay.

Our many sailing experiences taught us much about ourselves and our world. Creation is wonderfully predictable. The laws of physics work. Without the centerboard, a Snipe is extremely unstable and will not sail. In fact, without a centerboard—a keel on larger boats—no sailboat can tack into the wind, much less be stable enough for human visitors. The centerboard stabilizes the boat, provides the center of gravity, and enables the boat to tack at a forty-five-degree angle into the wind. Sailboats require centerboards.

Could creation be God's "centerboard," speaking to our listening hearts through the delicate balance of order and chaos? Could God's creative equilibrium, placed within God's creation, be an avenue to hear God's voice? The Scriptures speak to this issue. Remember the story of God's creative work as recorded in Genesis? "In the beginning when God created the heavens and the earth, the earth was a formless void and darkness covered the face of the deep, while a wind from God swept over the face of the waters" (1:1-2). God first created the heavens, and a formless and empty earth with which God fashioned all that is. Chaos was primary; order secondary. Yet, at the command of God, chaos and order sang a duet, praising God whose creative power worked in both to bring about reality as we know it. We call that reality the cosmos.

Into this cosmic garden, rooted in chaos and fashioned into order, God placed human beings to care for and "have dominion" over creation. Tragically, human beings have understood "dominion" as domination. The word actually means power, control, and understanding. God granted us dominion over creation not to crush it, but to witness and enjoy God's presence, power, and purposes through it.

For generations theologians have said God fashioned "cosmos out of chaos." I object. In reality, what we have is cosmos (reality) that is both chaos and order, brokenness and wholeness, ugliness and beauty, through which God can and does speak. Our responsibility and privilege are to listen for God's voice through the "that-ness" of creation in both its chaos and its order.

Illustrations abound. This tension may best be glimpsed in the life of Jesus. God granted the gift of free will to all persons who met Jesus of Nazareth in his earthly life. Fishermen chose to follow him; Pilate ordered his crucifixion. Created with choosing faculties, all who encountered Jesus acted as free persons in response to his message and mission. John loved Jesus; Herod considered him at best a nuisance.

What happened? Pilate ordered Jesus crucified, while Peter hid in fear. Even so, God revealed divine love in an unrepeatable, redemptive way through the suffering and death of Jesus. Human choice, coupled with cosmic order-chaos, resulted in the death of the Innocent One. Through that event, however, God revealed love that no human choice could then or now conquer. That revelation continues to be the very heartbeat of the Christian faith. The New Testament declares with one voice that human sin—the result of an age-old predisposition to disobey God repeated from generation to generation—could not eclipse or change the purposes of God.

In fact, God spoke through humanity's rejection of Jesus. If that is so—and I believe it is—then God still speaks through creation's order-chaos, human choice being a dynamic part of that reality. Are we listening? Are we tuning our hearts to hear the voice of God through the chaos and order of our world? For most of us, our problem is not God's silence, but our deafness. God is speaking. Yet we refuse to listen, or else we simply avoid the presence of God who persistently seeks a hearing in our lives. We need not suffer from spiritual deafness without relief. God's creation is still a powerful vehicle through which God speaks. Are we listening?

God's Voice in Chaos

Had polio not paid me a visit, I would not have known God in certain ways. Through the chaos of polio I came to experience God as faithful healer, disciplining parent, and unmovable presence. You ask: "You came to know God as faithful healer? You've said you walk with a limp—you've not been healed?" Yes, I have, but not physically. Physically, I've recovered from polio's insult. I will, however, always carry the limp polio left in its wake. Do you see it? Polio's work in my life did what polio does. No. God did not order polio to stalk the human family. As best I understand it, the virus we call polio is a mutation of God's creative work that came to be as the result of the freedom (chaos-order) God placed in creation. Such freedom is not without risks. To deny that freedom in creation is to deny that freedom in us all. That I cannot do.

Rather, I have come to experience God as healer through God's predictable chaos-order creation in another way. God gave me a gift. God placed within my life the ability to see polio for what it is. I could curse the virus or choose to see God's healing work at deeper levels in my life. Early on I fought the inevitable, cried buckets of tears because of my lot, and questioned God without mercy. Healing came—and still comes—when God's love broke through the pain and forced me to look more toward tomorrow than yesterday. I have since found healing in every sunrise, knowing the majesty of God can be seen as powerfully in chaos as in order. Radical healing came when I sensed God's invitation to look beyond what was to what could be. My whole perspective on life changed in that moment.

Second, through all of this, I've come to know God through the chaos as a disciplining parent. As a child, I didn't enjoy being disciplined. No child does. I had my share of spankings and deserved every one of them. By discipline, I don't mean punishment. Rather, God's discipline was packaged in braces and therapy. God's predictable creation, chaotic and orderly that it is, put me on notice that if I was going to maximize my minimum left leg, I was going to have to work.

Exercise, therapy, swimming, and sometimes pain were the tools God used to teach me physical discipline. Physical therapists worked with me for hours upon end. A man by the name of Johnny made my braces. A gifted orthopedic surgeon was my friend. All of them and many more were participants with me in God's healing. To a person, my parents included, none of them patronized me. They did their jobs; I was expected to do mine. Such is the stuff of discipline. Through their lives and my own experiences I met God as a disciplining parent. Can you see it? God invites us to act positively and faithfully in response to life as we meet it, not as we wish it would be. Whiners and gripers—if you choose to tune-in to them—can distort or even drown out the voice of God.

Finally, I came to know God through the chaos as an unmovable presence. God's presence is like a stone wall that does not move when we run into it. Like the aftereffects of polio, God doesn't change reality because life has changed for us. Chaos taught me that. Chaos taught me that, in the words of the prophet, God is like "a refiner's fire." God's fiery voice fires the mined ore of our lives—both the gold and the dross—with equal heat, refining the gold and removing the impurities. In that fire I have come to hear God's voice though wounded by creation's chaos.

Hearing God's voice in times when creation acts chaotic is no easy task. The late Swiss physician-therapist Paul Tournier, in his provocative book *Creative Suffering*, wrestled with the dynamic interplay of tragedy and human response. With pointed insight, he wrote: "What disturbs our lives, puts us out, irritates us, annoys us, affects us, makes us suffer—severely sometimes—does not make us grow and develop, but does make growth and development possible, on condition, of course, that we are not destroyed by it."[5] I believe God's voice speaks through the chaos of our lives, inviting us to grow and become more than we were before the tragedy-disaster-failure paid its untimely visit. Whether we grow and mature or atrophy and wilt, life is wrapped up in the choices we make in the midst of life's varied experiences.

God's Voice in Order

For some, order is the only place to meet God. Like a formal English garden, God is encountered as balanced order, symmetrical architecture, and fragrant beauty. In such a place all ugliness, dirt, and sin are banished. The birds sing, the gentle breezes blow, the predictable rains fall, and the whole of reality "makes sense." Like you, given the choice, I prefer hearing God's voice through the order and beauty of creation. And yes, like you, I savor "Kodak" moments in God's ordered, glorious world.

Five years ago, our family spent two weeks in Europe. One day we had an unplanned but never-to-be-forgotten surprise. The day was late. We had traveled from Venice, Italy, through Milan, and had just entered Switzerland. Our destination that evening was Interlocken. The map said we had another fifty kilometers to go. Even though the route was through the mountains—I had found a "shortcut"—we felt we could make it by dark.

Not! As we wound our way around a jagged mountain in the middle of Nowhere, Switzerland, we discovered the road ahead was closed due to repairs and wouldn't be open till the next morning. We came to a stop, reading the bad news. What would we do? Daylight was slipping away. Sleeping in the car was not an option. At that moment we remembered a little sign a few kilometers back that said "Edelweiss Hotel" (as in *The Sound of Music* song). We turned around, went back to the Edelweiss, and discovered the most beautiful place in God's world I've ever visited.

We spent the night in this ten-room hotel right out of "Heidi," rose to the sound of bells clanging from cows' necks, and enjoyed the best hot chocolate ever. The little village in which the Edelweiss was located had all of eight buildings in it. One of those buildings was a small Catholic church that may have held twenty. We didn't want to leave. Wherever we looked, in the middle of July, we saw snow-capped mountains. Nestled in this little valley was a slice of paradise and beauty we will remember for a lifetime.

You've had similar experiences—perhaps a sunrise in the desert, a summer evening in the Smoky Mountains, a fall walk in New England, or the sound of majestic music from your own backyard choir of cardinals, bluebirds, and sparrows. God surely speaks through the order of our world. Such communiqués remind us our lives can be as glorious if we will let go and savor these moments as gifts through which God speaks to those who are listening.

God's Voice in Balance

The listening heart learns to tune itself to hear God's voice through creation's chaos *and* order. Most of the time, however, God's voice speaks through *both*; we hear God's voice in the mix of creation's chaos and order. The sound of God's voice—syllables, words, phrases, sentences—is a mixed bag sounding of glory and terror, speaking to the listening heart.

Who among us does not prefer order, knowing as surely as we draw our next breath we will be called upon to deal with and respond to life in the midst of occasional chaos? As crazy as it sounds, we struggle more with making sense of life in the teeter-totter balance of order and chaos. When creation's chaos drowns our dreams in a flood, quick are some to announce God's judgment or question God's sovereignty. When success crowns hard work, snap pronouncements are made trumpeting the blessings of God. Difficult indeed is the task of carefully listening for God's voice when life is not so easily interpreted.

Life's "daily stuff" is our most challenging read. Like limp tea leaves wilting before the gaze of a fortuneteller, so are most of the days of our lives. We rise and ready ourselves for work, make our way to the office or the health club or the grocery store or the day-care center or the "whatever," do our assigned tasks, complete the day's demands, trudge home, and feed our hungry mouths. But alas, our soul's hunger is not satisfied . . . no malicious chaos today—disease, tragedy, loss–and no dazzling order–promotion, romance, rainbows—only daily stuff. It's the "dailies" such as rush-hour traffic, exercise routines, project deadlines, well-baby appointments, and grocery store errands that occupy much of our schedules. The question? How do we hear God's voice in creation's middle spaces, where neither chaos nor order overwhelms us?

Those who farm the land know the answer. Some years the rains come in abundance; other years drought dries up all that's been planted. Farmers who've tilled the earth for years can normally survive a bad year or two. Why? Because they know spring will come again and, perhaps next year, the rains will be more predictable and a bumper harvest will follow. Farmers keep farming, knowing chaos (drought) and order (gentle, frequent rains) are part of the agricultural package. "Daily stuff" for farmers is preparing the soil, sowing seed, replenishing the ground, and rising every morning to return to the fields and cultivate the crop.[6] Successful farmers are not overly excited by bumper crops nor totally discouraged by occasional droughts. The daily business of farming keeps them engaged in their work because they know nature's unpredictability (chaos) as well as nature's generosity (order).

So it must be with us. We are beneficiaries of a creation filled with messages from a loving and faithful God. We find ourselves born into creation through the chaos and order of a bloody birth. We discover our days to be—in all their glory and terror—scenes cast on creation's stage; we are born into a story already in progress and die into another story already going on.[7] Through every experience as participants in creation's order and chaos we have the opportunity to tune our hearts to hear the voice of God. To live fully, to seize our best humanity and highest God-created purposes, requires the heart's openness and receptivity. Such a listening heart in an otherwise noisy world knows this is God's world through which God's voice can be heard. The opportunity life affords us is to be engaged fully as participants in creation, ever listening for the sound of God's voice. Anxiety and fear are not productive responses to God's world; listening is.

Before you read on, take a morning, an afternoon, a starlit evening, or any combination of the above, and record your routines. Sit down with something to drink and perhaps a bowl of popcorn, and note beside each segment moments when you heard God's voice through God's creation. Where was it? Through the animal kingdom? The elements-weather-geography-topography of creation? Or some unexpected surprise over which you had no choice or control?

A second response to your list might be to note moments when you could have savored God's creation but forgot or refused to do so. How could those missed opportunities be teachable moments inviting you to tune your heart to perceive them in the future? Reflecting periodically on specific segments of a day is a powerful teaching tool. With God's creation as the instructor and your heart as the student, you can find lasting joys and powerful insights into living. The listening heart has still much to learn from God's fascinating and ever-changing world.

Notes

[1]In this chapter chaos means the seeming rebellion of creation observed most obviously in natural disasters and disease. This in no way refers to chaos theory as espoused by some within the scientific community. The chaos of which I speak is the same phenomenon to which Paul refers in Romans 8:18-23 when he describes creation as groaning. On the other hand, order refers to the beauty, harmony, and wonder of creation. Whereas our natural response to chaos is frustration and even fear, our natural response to order is delight and even worship.

[2]John David Weaver, *In the Beginning God: Modern Science and the Christian Doctrine of Creation*, Regent's Study Guides 3 (Macon GA: Smyth & Helwys Publishing, Inc., 1994) 68. Though beyond the boundaries of our study on prayer, a thoughtful reading of Weaver's book would place one in the midst of the current scientific debate about design, order, and purpose in creation.

[3]Dennis Farney, "Natural Questions: Chaos Theory Seeps into Ecology Debate Stirring Up a Tempest," *The Wall Street Journal*, Vol. 224, No. 6 (11 July 1994) A-1.

[4]Paul Davies, *The Mind of God* (London: Penguin Books, 1992) is one of many physicists-mathematicians-cosmologists who, though not a believer, sees observable design in the universe. Others writing in this field are Stephen Hawking, Douglas Adams, J. D. Barrow, and Richard Dawkins.

[5]Paul Tournier, *Creative Suffering* (San Francisco: Harper & Row Publishers, 1981) 131-32.

[6]Jesus had something to say about the mystery of life's daily routines and our response to them. In one of his parables, recorded in Mark 4:26-29, Jesus spoke of the faithful farmer sowing seed and then waiting for the seed to germinate, grow, and produce a harvest. In the parable, however, between sowing and reaping—a time when ancient farmers did nothing—the farmer anxiously inspects a phenomenon that is in no way affected by his observations. Rather, the seed's growth to maturity is a mystery affected only by the farmer's sowing and creation's gift of rain. The harvest is in no way affected by the farmer's anxiety. His job between sowing and reaping is to await the ripening of the grain, not to inspect anxiously—daily?—the crop's progress.

[7]I am indebted to Canon Herbert O'Driscoll for this insight spoken during a sermon he delivered at the College of Preachers, Washington DC, 1992.

Chapter 3

GOD'S WORD—HUMAN WORDS

The Bible has held a central place in my life for as long as I can remember. I received a Bible when my mother enrolled me in the cradle roll of our church. As a child I remember bringing my Bible to church, reading the Bible at home, learning about the Bible in Sunday School, and hearing ministers preach sermons from the Bible. For Christians, the Bible is the Book of books. Year after year, more Bibles are published and purchased around the world than any other book.

What is it about the Bible that invites us into a relationship with God? Does the Bible speak the words of God to us? If so, how are we to understand them, interpret them, and find them meaningful in our lives? Many today, by their own confession, suffer from a form of functional illiteracy when it comes to the Bible. Is it so with you? A Bible occupies some space under a coffee table at home or on a dusty bookshelf at the office, but you could no more quickly find the book of Nehemiah than walk on water. You have a Bible, but the Bible has little of you.

The Gallup organization tells us that more and more Americans are hungry for firsthand knowledge of the Bible. Bible studies abound across our country. If you ask around, you'll probably find a study going on at your place of work during lunch or in your neighborhood. We are not groping in the fog of biblical illiteracy because of a shortage of Bibles or Bible studies.

What gives? How could a nation whose fundamental laws flow out of the Judeo-Christian biblical stream be so ignorant of and, quite frankly, turned off by the Bible? You may be one who has wanted to know more about the Bible, but been overwhelmed by its sheer size and the difficult and hard-to-understand language and arrangement of the Bible. Why are persons who want to enjoy the Bible as a companion to their soul's longing for God so indifferent to it?

One answer has to do with the millions of Americans who are turned off to the message of the Bible because many who carry Bibles are often obnoxious, belligerent, and shallow. When some who claim to be Christian bomb abortion clinics and murder doctors in the name of God and the Bible, thinking citizens are justifiably outraged. On a more familiar front, in community after community, some aggressive Christians, "preaching the Word," beat people over the heads with their own interpretation of the Bible. In so doing, the very Bible that communicates the love and acceptance of God is perceived by those outside the faith to be a book whose purpose is to beat people into submission. Such preaching is, no doubt, offered sincerely, but its overbearing style turns many off to the larger message of the Bible.

Others are turned off to God and the Bible by some of the events recorded in the Bible that do not square with their own sense of decency or morality. Recently a thoughtful woman made an appointment to talk with me about her faith journey. I listened for nearly an hour as she shared her understanding of God from the Bible she knew. She was—as you may be—particularly turned off by the brutality pictured in the Old Testament. As I listened, I found myself agreeing with some of her critique of God as portrayed in the Bible as she understood it. After awhile I said, "If I believed the person of God was as you described Him, I wouldn't believe in God either." Her entire picture of God revealed a deity of anger, indifference, judgment, and punishment. My friend is not alone. Many people have the same perception of God, gleaned from the little bits of the Bible they have read or heard summarized by others.

Let's stop for a moment. Ask yourself: Have I read the Bible? I ask this question because many who are turned off by the Bible have never seriously read it. Their Bible knowledge is derived secondhand from the Bible's critics, opponents, defenders, or a dissonant mix of all three. Honestly, have you taken the time to read selective Psalms, the Gospel of John, the fortieth chapter of the prophet Isaiah, 1 Corinthians 13, or the Sermon on the Mount (Matt 5-7)?

I'm reminded of a man who once told me the church I serve as pastor is "liberal, cold, and full of rich people." I listened and then asked, "Have you visited our church, participated in a worship service, or talked with active members of the church?" He dropped his head and said, "No, I haven't." "In all honesty," I replied, "you owe it to yourself to check out the church you are verbally destroying before you make such sweeping judgments." He agreed and later joined the church! We call such unfounded opinion prejudice. Many today hold negative prejudices toward the Bible.

I ask again: Have you read the Bible and, in reading the Bible, honestly attempted to listen to the voice of God speaking to you? Did you read it and follow up your reading by having a conversation with a trusted friend whose faith is rooted in a relationship with God as revealed in the Bible? Through the centuries of human history, in nation after nation, among people as diverse as the stars of the sky, the Bible has been an instrument through which the voice of God has spoken.

Perhaps you're asking: How can I read the Bible and, in reading its human words, discover God's voice addressing me in my need and answering my questions? I, too, have asked that question for most of my life. I spent the better part of twelve years pursuing educational goals to enable me to understand the message and meaning of the Bible. Every day I find myself reading portions of the Bible and asking: What does this mean? What difference do these words make in my life? How can this text open my being to a fuller experience of God and others?

Let's face these questions honestly. Moving in the direction of answering our questions requires us first to consider how *not* to read the Bible. Frankly, many fall into Bible-reading traps from which they never recover. When the Bible is approached as anything less than a mystery out of which we hear the voice of God, biblical ignorance and/or indifference can grow and suffocate the listening heart.

The Four Traps

The first snare into which Bible readers fall is the trap of *isolationism*. That is, they isolate a verse here and a verse there, throw them together, and come up with "the way." Taken to its extreme, this is the interpretive method of sectarian religion, cults, and religious fanaticism. I'm reminded of the story about the preacher who believed God's direction came best when he threw open the Bible in a couple of places, pointed his finger at a verse, and delivered an extemporaneous sermon based on the verses so identified. This worked well until one day he threw open the Bible to the verse that reads: "Judas went and hanged himself." Needing a bit more Bible for a sermon, he plopped the Bible back down, dropped his finger, and read, "Go and do likewise."

This method does not work. Unfortunately, much of our theology is isolationist in nature. A verse from Genesis is tied by one word to a verse in Luke that is interpreted by a verse in Revelation. Mix this cake together, throw it in the narrow-minded oven of fundamentalism or liberalism, and almost anything can be justified by the Bible. The Bible is not a book of verses one strings together to make sense of life. The Bible is a collection of stories, poetry, hymns, and history through which the eternal God is revealed to humanity. Stories contain verses, but stories are whole expressions of the experience of God in the lives of people.

To read the Bible as if it were a confusing tome of isolated verses needing the human mind to put it all together is to diminish the power of the Bible and shortchange the gift the Bible is to our lives. Falling into the trap of isolationism is a less-than-ideal way to discover the voice of God speaking through the pages of the Bible.

A second trap into which we can fall is the trap of *truth-finding*. That is, one approaches the Bible as a treasure chest of "truths" discovered only by the faithful. These truths, more often than not, are revealed under the leadership of a revered and godly teacher or preacher. Sadly, this teaching method often fosters a dependency upon the revered teacher whose writings and utterances are considered by the faithful as, or nearly as, inspired as the Scriptures.

Let's be honest. All who study the Bible—both the "armchair" student and the seasoned scholar—are dependent upon others for insights, guidance, and inspiration. Good teaching always creates a bond between teacher and student. This bonding between the teacher and student, writer and reader, scholar and neophyte, is dynamic in its power to challenge our presuppositions, inform our perspectives, and inspire further study. This healthy and stimulating bond between teacher and student is the fuel that stokes our mind's fire for mining the riches of God's Word.

Unfortunately, some teachers present the findings of their study in such a way as to suggest theirs is the only way or the only "right" or "spiritual" insight into a particular passage or theological concept. When this occurs, truth-finding becomes an end in itself, and the revered teacher becomes the sole truth-finder. This mind-set all too often turns a student's hunger for learning into a dependence upon the teacher.

The situation among persons trapped in this way of approaching the Bible is predictable. For example, some Bible students will not read a book by an unfamiliar author until their pastor or a revered teacher's review of the book and the author is considered. Why? The writer may be "a liberal." Truth-finders had best position a writer before reading his/her book, evaluate all God-talk in light of the "truth" already found, and then decide whether or not any new insights into the Scriptures will be considered.

I must ask: Is the Bible a book of truths awaiting our discovery? In an ultimate sense, the Bible reveals the Truth of all reality as revealed in the person of Jesus Christ. Jesus, the divine Son, said: "I am the way, and the truth, and the life" (John 14:6). Even so, is the purpose and intent of the Bible to nestle truths within its pages so we can discover them? Do we hear the voice of God through the Bible's pages embarked on a truth-finding mission? I say no. The Bible is filled with countless truths that confront the thoughtful reader. My problem lies in the area of method. I submit it is possible to spend a lifetime mining truths from the Bible and never encounter the reality of God who is the Truth.

For example, anyone who has fallen in love knows you don't fall in love with the truth of love. You fall in love with a person, and in relationship with that person you find yourself living into the truth of love. Only naive newlyweds fall in love with the truth of having a baby. In reality, parents love the baby and, in so doing, discover the wonderful truths about life glimpsed through dimpled cheeks and dirty diapers. Life's greatest "truths" are not studied; they are experienced. So it is with God. Finding a "truth" about God is a cheap substitute for knowing God and hearing God's voice.

A third snare into which Bible readers easily fall is the *question-and-answer* trap. Simply put, this trap suggests the Bible is God's "answer book" to my questions. There is a kernel of truth to this approach. Like you, I've often discovered life-changing answers to difficult and disturbing questions in my reading of the Bible. Is the Bible, however, a divine answer book? Of course not!

Read the Bible, and you will discover person after person who, like you, walked away from an encounter with God with more questions unanswered than answered. Jacob wrestled with an angel all night and limped away into a risky future still wondering what the twists and turns of his life meant. Jesus knelt in the Garden of Gethsemane and later rose to his feet with questions God chose not to answer. Listen to Jesus' question from the cross: "My God, my God, why have you forsaken me?" (Matt 27:46). Heaven was silent; his question unanswered.

No wonder many have come to the Bible and limped away in anger, confusion, and loneliness. If you've thought the Bible had to have an answer to all your questions, you have known more than your share of disappointment. The Bible reveals many answers to life's questions, but its purpose, as best I can say, is not to fire back answers like a computer to our endless string of questions. As we read the Bible listening for the voice of God, we discover through the Bible's stories, poetry, and teaching the reality of God who speaks and asks not a few questions of us.

A final pit into which Bible readers can fall is the *learning-knowledge* trap. Our country is not starving for a lack of Bible studies, theological seminaries, religious books, or educated clergy.

In many churches, week after week, prepared teachers stand before classes and teach a Sunday School lesson. For many, the lesson taught is the culmination of hours of study, pouring over the Bible, referencing commentaries, studying maps, perhaps even using the original languages.

Having said that, learning the history, language, literary forms, and theological contours of the Bible is not the same endeavor as listening for the voice of God through reading the Bible. They are two distinctively different pursuits. Quite honestly, the majority of universities, seminaries, and divinity schools have well-trained, committed professors whose academic study of religion has equipped them to teach. Knowing the facts about the Bible, considering the history of the Bible, even learning well the subject matter within the Bible is not the same as listening to the God of the Bible.

Just as we can attend church and never experience God, so we can attend Sunday School, master a study guide, learn all we can learn about the Bible, God, the church, and theology, and never encounter or be encountered by God. Many do. Why? Because the quest for knowledge (facts) can seduce us into missing and even avoiding the larger and more risky experience of being in relationship with God. For example, you can spend less than $100 on some excellent books and videotapes describing the city of Rome. In fact, you could become an expert on Roman history, architecture, and so forth, and never visit Rome. Experiencing Rome, however, requires the expense of getting there, the time required in traveling, and the intellectual-spiritual risk of discovering a Rome that is, in reality, different from the Rome of your study. Having done both, I'll take a trip to Rome any day over studying a book about Rome.

So it is with all four traps into which we can fall in studying the Bible. Isolationism, truth-finding, answers-to-my-questions, and learning have many good qualities about them. They fall short, way short, of an encounter with God through the experience of reading the Bible and listening for the voice of God. To that task we now turn.

Reading as Listening

A person who sits down with a Bible and begins to read it as a novel from cover to cover is in for a major disappointment. Yes, I've known people who have worked through the Bible from beginning to end. They deserve a medal! In all my years of living within the pages of the Bible, I've never read "the whole thing" from cover to cover. Nevertheless, I suppose I've read the Bible in its entirety several times in the course of personal study and sermon preparation.

How then can a person read the Bible and, in the experience of reading, hear the voice of God? Let's form an answer to that question around three words: text, plan, and purpose. First, you need to purchase a contemporary text of the Bible. Many people die on their third page of Bible reading, harpooned by the language of the King James Version. I might as well say it now and be done with it: there is nothing sacred about the King James Version of the Bible. It did not exist prior to 1611! What many people find holy about the King James translation is its Shakespearean style, eloquent phrasing, and "holy-sounding" language. For many, the King James Version is God's Word because that's the text they heard read around the dinner table or from the pulpit. For others, a beloved pastor preached from the King James Version and occasionally lambasted "modern translations." Having said that, vast numbers of serious Christians honestly believe that any version of the Bible other than the King James is either wrong, corrupt, or both.

Relax! Buy a contemporary translation of the Bible. Popular contemporary translations include the *New International Version*, *The New Revised Standard Version*, the *American Standard Version*, and the new *Contemporary English Version*. There is no perfect translation. Translation is not an exact science and by necessity passes through fallible human instruments. Buy a contemporary translation for reading purposes—read God's Word, and listen for God's voice. You will find God speaking to you in profound ways when you start reading God's Word in a contemporary translation. That was the genius of the King James Version in the seventeenth century—people heard God's word in the language of their day. That same dynamic works in our day when a listening heart picks up a contemporary translation of the Bible and begins to read.[1]

Second, develop a plan for reading the Bible. A good place to begin your reading is the book at the center of the Bible, the Psalms. In fact, a simple plan for reading the Bible is to go to the center and work your way out. Genesis (particularly the first eleven chapters) and Revelation are considered by many to be the two most difficult books of the Bible to understand. Read them last! Start in the Psalms, any one of them (there are 150). There you will meet people who wrote of their soul's anguish, confusion, anger, and celebration. Every human emotion can be found in the Psalms.

If you're wanting to read stories, start working through the Gospel of Luke and read the life of Jesus. Luke contains some of Jesus' most remembered parables. From the Old Testament, read the story of God's relationship with Abraham beginning in Genesis 12. Keep reading and see what happened to his and Sarah's only child, Isaac. Don't stop. The intriguing, dysfunctional relationships revealed in Isaac and Rebekah's marriage spill over into their twin sons, Esau and Jacob. Turn to the New Testament and read one of Paul's letters (Philippians and Ephesians would be a good start) or the Letter of James. Listen and you'll be amazed at what God says to you through these human words.

Through it all, our purpose in reading is listening. Because of that, it's okay to begin reading at a place in the Bible where human beings like yourself were listening for God's voice as they faced the very difficulties you are facing now. When you discover the Bible's ability to "scratch" your soul's spiritual "itch," you will be hooked on reading it and soon will find yourself asking, Why did I avoid this book for so long?

Third, read the Bible with a clear purpose in mind. As you read, ask: What is God saying to me through this psalm, or this parable, or this story from Jesus' life? Your purpose is devotional, not academic. I say again, there is a place for the academic study of the Bible. Yes, often God breaks through my study of a Greek verb or some theological puzzle in clear and arresting ways. More times than not, however, I find myself listening to God's voice as I read passages from the Bible for the sheer joy of reading and listening. I invite you to make the same discovery.

With text, plan, and purpose clearly in focus, how does one hear the voice of God through reading the Word of God? First, a caution. Remember as you read that every person whose name appears in the Bible is spiritually much like you. Bible readers often get infected with the "saint virus." The people who populate the Bible may be considered saints, but while they were walking the earth, they were very human and subject to the same weaknesses, temptations, and failures all of us face.

Adam and Eve were the Bible's first humans to walk the earth, but they were not the last human beings to experience temptation, sin, guilt, and judgment. One doesn't have to live very long to know the reality of being thrown out of paradise. Too soon the honeymoon's passion is interrupted by two-car payment, high mortgage, career-demanding, consumer-hungry stress. All of us know to varying degrees the thick fog of guilt that suffocates us when forbidden fruit is tasted. Their story is my story, your story, and our story.

Second, read the Bible as a discoverer. No one has a corner on the meaning and message of the Bible. Persons who "have arrived" in the land of Bible knowledge are often dwarfed by their own success. Winning the game of "Bible Trivia" does not mean one has succeeded in being mastered by the message and God of the Bible.

As a child, I participated in the Baptist program we used to call "Sword Drill." Several children would form a straight line in front of an adult who would say, "Attention . . . draw swords (our Bibles) . . . Acts 16:31." The first child who found it, marked it, and stepped forward won that round of the Sword Drill. It was great fun and taught us to master the order of the books of the Bible and to be able to locate Bible passages quickly and with confidence. I happen to believe Sword Drill was and still is a good idea. Unfortunately, some people live their whole lives with a Sword Drill mentality. The Bible is not read to discover the mysterious voice of God, but rather to confirm the voice of God heard long ago in Sunday School or from a persuasive preacher.

The listening heart finds the Bible to be a faithful witness to God's voice. To listen *for* the voice of God is to discover God breaking into our lives, often in surprising and uncomfortable ways, to inform our present, interpret our past, and challenge our future. No doubt about it, God has spoken to my life through hundreds of teachers, preachers, and previous journeys into the Bible. I am, like you, grateful for every moment in which I've discovered God's voice in times past. Those past discoveries, however, must not be allowed to cripple or mute today's discovery of God's voice through the reading of God's Word.

Kathie and I have three children. All teenagers, we recently replayed a videotape of them we made several years ago on vacation. My oldest son, like his younger brother, has had a major voice change in the last five years. You know what happened. Nathan couldn't believe he was hearing his voice on the tape. That *was* his voice (no kidding, Nathan!). The person was the same, but the voice had changed with the changing of time. So it is with God. God is the same yesterday, today, and forever. In reading the Bible, however, we find God's voice changing in its inflection, tone, and cadence. To read the Bible as a discoverer is to hear the voice of God anew, alive, powerful, and persuasive in this moment of our lives. God is the same, but time and circumstances force us to hear God's voice as if for the first time.

Finally, listen to the Bible as a beggar. How hungry are you for an encounter with God? In more than twenty years of ministry, I've observed one unchanging reality in the lives of people: the more destitute the life, the more shattered the dreams, the more hungry the heart. When your health is excellent, your stocks up, your business successful, your children happy, your mate fulfilled, and life, as our Brazilian friends say, is "all blue skies," you have little hunger for God. In our self-made, precariously insecure success we easily convey the unspoken "Who needs God?"

Life's order can and often does move in the direction of chaos. When chaotic life crashes down around us–as it does eventually for everyone–our souls hunger for a word from God. When we read the

Bible, we read as hungry beggars listening for God's voice and discovering in our listening God's presence. In honest moments we must confess we are all beggars in the spirit. All of us are clothed in death's rags. We know firsthand a growling, scratching soul hunger that can only be satisfied by feasting on Living Bread.

A great discovery awaits you when you pick up the Bible and begin to read it as a hungry, questing beggar. You will find human beings whose names are different, but whose lives are much like your own. Listen to their stories. Hear the agony of David as he mourns the death of Absalom. Witness the daring of Ruth. Stare at the cowardice of Peter. Bow in the presence of the overwhelming humility of Mary. Through it all, through your many readings and your periodic ventures into the narrative world of the Bible, listen for the voice of God and, in listening, find your heart drawn into a presence that is the very life of God.

Notes

[1]Translations of the New Testament by individuals are also delightful to read and study. A few of the more exceptional works would include New Testament translations by Helen Montgomery, Charles Williams, J. B. Phillips, and the paraphrase by Eugene Peterson, *The Message*.

Chapter 4
PEOPLE OF GOD—FAITHFUL PEOPLE

God's world and God's Word are trusted partners in our active listening to God's voice. These gifts from God are partners who, like sentinels, refuse to allow our souls to suffocate in the noise of this present age. The world and the Word call us to seize every listening opportunity. A third partner awaits our discovery. This third partner is the company of others who bear their witness to God's faithfulness. The faithful community of others—young and old, wise and foolish, male and female, singing and speaking—gather around us as God's witnesses to touch our being with the gift of spiritual companionship.

This faithful community counts among its number both the living and the dead. Among the living, the faithful community is met in predictable places such as churches and synagogues, Bible study groups, sensitive friends, and trusted confidants. The dead, now silent in life, still speak through the media of literature, tapes, the visual arts, and music. Together the faithful community becomes a chorus of affirmation and power inviting us to hear what they have heard, to feel what they have felt, and to become in faith what they have and are becoming.

In *The Book of Common Prayer*, the collection of faithful words that have sustained an entire community of believers for more than four centuries, the marriage rite concludes with this petition. "Grant that the bonds of our common humanity, by which all your children are united one to another, and the living to the dead, may be so transformed by your grace, that your will may be done on earth as it is in heaven."[1] So it is for all who listen for God's voice. The faithful community present on earth now and those who have gone before us in death speak a powerful reminder to us that God is speaking. We can listen if we will.

The Bible beckons us to live and pray in communion with others who know God in Christ. Jesus' Model Prayer begins with the words "Our Father."[2] Throughout that prayer of prayers words tie our lives to those who pray with us. Here they are:

> Give *us* this day our daily bread;
> Forgive *us* our trespasses as
> *we* forgive *those* who trespass against *us*;
> And lead *us* not into temptation,
> but deliver *us* from evil. (KJV) (italics mine)

Just as Jesus taught us to voice our petitions in community, so also we are summoned to hear God's voice in and through the faithful community that bears its witness to Christ as Lord. God's gathered and forgiven witness to God's love has been and still is the body of Christ, the church.

Right now you may be expecting a hard-sell invitation to church. Relax! The church is the more visible—may I say obvious?—community of faithful life partners. Like blooming dogwood trees in a native forest, America's landscape is dotted with churches. In some communities, mainline churches and their sectarian offspring have multiplied in confusing numbers. One doesn't have to live long someplace, however, to know firsthand that the multiplied dozens of churches do not a healthy community make. Tragically, churches cannot and do not always live up to their Christ-centered billing. Like the changing of the tides, church attendance in America is up one decade and down the next. Those longing for the "good old days" may be shocked to discover that American church attendance was a scant 16 percent in 1850!

Attending church, however, has little to do with being the church and discovering within the institution of the church God's faithful people. Each week millions of people with whom we work drift into church—some a different one each week looking for that special place or caring person—hungry to hear and be embraced by a love greater than they can find in some local bar or dance club. The painful truth is, the number would stretch easily into the millions of persons—you may be one—who slipped into a church, looked around for some soul-friendship, reached out for the smallest kind of help, and met rejection. As a pastor, I grieve over those who walk into the space I call "church" and leave untouched by God and/or God's people. No church is free from this tragedy. It repeats itself, even in the warmest of churches, week after week.

In the face of this reality, we must ask: Why do I need the faithful community anyway? Aren't God's world and God's Word enough? How can I find God's faithful community today? Who and where are the people who are seeking to live their lives in faithful ways? How does my relationship to others in a faith community enable and empower me to hear God's voice? These are good questions and good places to begin.

Who Needs 'Em Anyway?

A number of years ago—I was a teenager at the time—one of my Dad's friends stopped attending the church where we were members. Weeks passed, and Dad finally called him. I've changed his name, but this is a faithful re-creation of their conversation. "Charlie, I haven't seen you at church recently. Where have you been?" After a few moments of uncomfortable maneuvering, the man finally spoke. "Neal," he said reluctantly, "they said they didn't want me there anymore." Thinking quickly, my dad responded with these probing words. "Charlie, did Jesus say that?" "No, Neal, Jesus didn't say that." The man came back to church. Permit me to brag a moment on my dad. In that conversation he modeled the faithful community to a friend. That's not to say my dad, anymore than you or I, has always modeled the faithful community. None of us bat a thousand! At that moment, however, when Dad called his friend, asked a good question sensitively, and simply was "there," he expressed a concern and faithfulness consonant with the life and love of Christ.

All of us—yes, even ministers—have asked ourselves, "Who needs 'em anyway?" It may be the most sinister question believers ever ask. The church and church people can be maddeningly frustrating at times. For some, the church experience has left thick scar tissue. Some off-handed remark made by an unthinking church member wounded your heart when you were a teenager. The years have passed, you've lived what you said—"I'll *never* go back to church!"—and a mountain of scar tissue has grown over a once small but still painful wound.

For many, the word church is like the word dentist. I'm grateful for my dentist. Truth is, in this present season of my life, I have an excellent dentist. But dentist was not a positive word in my growing-up years. I am still paying for the dental sins of my childhood. Today I'd be in dentures had it not been for good dental care in my adult years. My discomfort with dentists growing up was "lived through" and "outgrown" because of a higher goal: good dental hygiene.

Spiritually, our lives require faithful care. Yes, at times the church lets all its children down. Face it! There are no perfect churches, or perfect pastors, or always-totally sensitive, giving church members. The fact is, the sooner we accept the church as a community of human beings whose "sin status" has been named, but not obliterated, the sooner we will find ourselves slipping back into the church. Who needs 'em? You do, I do, we all need a community of faithful others. Why?

First, God's created world and living Word find faithful interpreters in the lives of people who've lived in and with both for a long time. Without the faithful witness of God's people, I would have folded my spiritual tent a long time ago. In my early years polio devastated my health and not a few dreams of my parents. In those moments the world where polio stalked children unchecked was the enemy, and God's Word, though loved, was terribly silent. My parents would be the first to tell you it was the faithful community of love at our church who prayed for us, loved us, and by their presence and many gifts of hope told us we would all get through that tragedy together. The faithful community spoke the words of God when the other two partners—both world and Bible—were suspect and confusing.

Second, God's world and God's Word form the background and reminder that God's faithful people have listened and responded to God's voice through the ages. You'll remember we wrestled with the unpredictable, confusing dimension of creation earlier. It is the Bible that reminds us that faithful people lived through all kinds of difficult and impossible-to-explain physical disasters. Herbert O'Driscoll, in his book *Emmanuel: Encountering Jesus as Lord*, echoes Donald Allchin's insight into what Allchin calls the "community in time" across the ages with whom we share faith.[3] Their witness to

God's faithfulness *then* is like the faithful witness of God's people *now*. Their faithful witness is an instrument through which God speaks to our lives, telling us, with God's world and Word, we have not been cosmically abandoned to a mindless fate.

Where Are They?

You can find God's people almost anywhere. I've found faithful believers in such diverse places as bars, city parks, middle-of-the-night coffee shops, bridge clubs, golf courses, day-care centers, offices, garages, *and* churches! Please don't interpret my comment as a criticism of the church. To the contrary, I say what all of us know to be true and many of us have been afraid to express: the church as institution—name, address, building, programs, budgets, boards, ministers—must not be equated with the church as faithful community. We can and normally do find God's faithful people within the environs of the institutional church, but such discovery is not always a sure thing.

You may have heard the story of the man who, following a moving sermon, came forward in a church to confess his faith in Christ and ask for church membership. The man was a notorious sinner, whose third marriage had ended because of his abusive behavior. Finally, grace crashed through his angry heart. He realized his only way through the disaster of his life was with Christ's help.

When the minister presented him to the church, the people, knowing his past, refused to accept him for membership. Dejected, the man walked out the door of the church and sat down on the front steps to talk with God. "Lord, I came asking your people to accept me, and they voted me down." After a moment of heavenly silence, God spoke. "Mike, don't let it bother you. I've been trying unsuccessfully to get in that church for years!" At times the church as institution does not act like Christ.

A steeple, pews, a preacher, and an organ do not a church make. Even so, a high probability exists that you will find God's faithful community within an organized church fellowship. I am blessed beyond words with the gift of serving a church that is both institutionally and spiritually big. Neither pastor nor people are perfect, but the fellowship that calls me "pastor" has within its institutional walls a larger, caring, and serving body of believers. What a gift! If you are struggling with this, remember God's faithful community is discovered in relationship, not religion; in encounter, not membership; in serving, not observing.

Listening for God's voice is all about a relationship with God and God's people that leads to a way of life. If your religion is not anchored in meaningful, life-enriching relationships that draw strength from God and focus life around God, you've embraced an idea, not the living God. Devoid of a dynamic relationship with Christ, Christianity, filled as it is with revolutionary ideas, is nothing more than a "do-gooders" club in a world where many good clubs are doing many good things.

Week after week guests visiting our worship services or Bible study hour tell me how well they were received and how surprised they are that a "big" church could be so warm. Such reports about our fellowship please me to no end. Nevertheless, at least once a month, I'll call on a recent visitor who will say words I've heard my entire ministry. "Nobody spoke to me. I walked in, sat down, 'enjoyed' the service, but not a soul said a word to me."

I apologize and ask the person to give us another chance and, when he/she returns, come by the door and allow me the privilege of putting a face to the voice on the phone. As the conversation ends and I put the receiver back in its cradle, I can't help but wonder whether the guest made eye contact with anyone, spoke to anyone, sat by anyone, or entered into the experience of worship to any meaningful degree. Forgive my skepticism. I know there are churches where guests extend warm hands and are met by cold stares. Believe me. Such churches exist. If you want to find God's faithful community, however, you have a responsibility to engage yourself to the same degree you expect others to engage you. A little eye contact, a brief visit with the minister at the door asking for an appointment, and genuinely participating in the hour of worship will do wonders for your quest for community.

This "relationship versus religion" dichotomy is just as real away from the institutional church as within it. All across our community, and I suspect yours as well, business people meet weekly in prayer and Bible study groups. Where I live most of these groups are non-denominational. Baptists, Methodists, Catholics, Presbyterians, Episcopalians, and others get together in a break room, a restaurant, or each other's homes to pray, study the Bible, and be with each other as God's faithful community. Relationships are the key. Ask around where you live or work, and you'll find a group or groups of faithful believers who are serious about listening to God in their lives. God's faithful community can be found almost anywhere if you, the seeker, are willing to risk a little in order to discover meaningful relationships with others.

What Can I Expect?

Expectations are the spotlights that emphasize our feelings in relationships. Imagine your life is a drama. As one scene slips into another, the spotlight of expectation draws your attention from one careless remark said offhandedly by a friend, to a health disappointment, and later to a surprising happiness. What you expected to see or experience in any one scene or act was missed. You threw the spotlight of expectation on one corner of the stage while the plot-turning action was happening in the shadows. For example, you review the three-year illness of your mother as it moved from diagnosis to death. You expected loneliness, throwing the spotlight of your emotions on your own fear, anxiety, and pain. In the shadows, however, faithful friends, church members, and neighbors were reaching out to you, helpless and at times rejected because of your own isolating grief. You expected loneliness and found it, even as others were offering companionship.

How often have I heard married couples describe in dirty detail each other's faults and sins. The spotlight of expectation is thrown on the wrong, the flaw, the inconsistency, rather than on the larger stage of fidelity, passion, and dreams that wait in the shadows for expectation's spotlight to shine once again on them.

On the other hand, expectation's spotlight can be a wonderful gift. Look at the stage again. You expected to rear healthy, balanced, loving children—and you did! You expected your home to be loving, and you made it that way. You expected to find faithful friends in the church, and you found them even as they found you. I believe the key to all successful and enduring relationships is this controllable bright light we call expectations. I've not done a scientific survey, but experience tells me the masses avoid the church not because they don't need the company of faithful believers. Quite the contrary. If you've avoided the church because of a negative experience in your younger years or because you've pegged the church to be something it's not, look again at your expectations.

Positively, knowing better than most the ever-present faults of the church, I lift up four "A's" you can discover among God's faithful community. First, shine the light of expectation on the word *acceptance*. Caption the entire life of Jesus Christ from his birth to his death and resurrection with the word acceptance. Someone has said you know a person's character by his enemies. Jesus' critics said of him, "He eats with tax collectors and sinners." Jesus accepted the likes of uneducated fishermen, businessmen, teachers, political activists, the terminally ill, streetwalkers, and common criminals into his community of love.

The same is true for those who faithfully follow Jesus Christ today. Walk into a church anywhere in the world, look into the eyes of those who gather there, communicate to them you are seeking to hear and know God, and you will find open arms of acceptance. It is part of the Christian nature to accept others as Christ has accepted us. Moving toward the faithful community will expose you to a level of acceptance unlike any you have known before. Alcoholics Anonymous has radically changed the way we look at addiction and dependency. The founders of AA were believers who themselves had suffered at their own hands the dehumanizing effects of poor choices. The very foundation of AA rests upon the idea that in a group of alcoholics, *all* are accepted the way they come through the door. That is the invitation Christ offers to all who seek to hear and know the voice of God. The hymn we love to sing, "Just as I am without one plea, but that Thy blood was shed for me," is the hymn the church embodies. Come as you are—you are accepted.

Now turn the spotlight of expectation to the word *acknowledgment*. The faithful community of believers in a church or a Bible study or prayer group will acknowledge your questions and your faith journey. Like any large institution, the church has its share of bad press perpetrated by the few to the anguish of the many. One negative impression given to many outside the church by a few inside the church is the "know-it-all" myth. Some mistakenly expect the church to be a place where questions are not welcome, answers are all "Yes" and "No" (mostly "No"), and the journey of faith is a narrow path known only by the few and led by an infallible, charismatic preacher.

Not so! If you're seeking to hear and know God's voice, you will find faithful partners within the church who will acknowledge your questions by taking them seriously. At the end of each service at my church I invite people to sit down with a minister or layperson and have a conversation about the journey of faith. That's what Jesus did. Read the four Gospels, and you'll meet a Savior who engaged people in conversation along the seashore, in the marketplace, at the house of worship, in homes, and beside the highway. The Gospels are filled with scores of questions people put to Jesus. Without exception, Jesus received their questions with a sensitivity and openness that invited the questioner into a deeper dialogue about faith.

You can and should expect God's faithful people to acknowledge your questions as an important part of your own faith journey. The church at its best is not a repository of answers spoken by know-it-all believers, but a community of living, questioning, caring people who have a relationship with God in Christ. Candidly, the longer I follow Jesus, the more questions I have. A relationship with Christ does not promise a life filled with answers, but rather gives life a faith-foundation for honest questions. Seen through the eyes of faith, all questions take on new possibilities. It is the faithful community that poses questions to the larger human family. Faithful believers ask: Why are human beings still dying of starvation when the world can more than provide for all its inhabitants? Is "getting ahead" the ultimate goal of human life? Is there more to being human than the pursuit of "life, liberty, and happiness?" The list is endless. Suffice it to say, the faithful community is composed of persons who will acknowledge your faith journey as one in which they too participate. Such companionship opens our lives to listen for God's voice.

Third, turn expectation's spotlight on the word *affirmation*. Just as two molecules of hydrogen and one molecule of oxygen form water, so acceptance and acknowledgment thrown together in a faithful community result in affirmation. Like the pungent fragrance of a rose, affirmation perfumes all relationships. God's faithful community is where one hears God's "Yes" to life. Where acceptance embraces the person, affirmation embraces the person's dreams. Look again at your life's drama. Review the times you felt as if you could conquer the world. Turn up the light of affirmation on that scene, and you will relive a spiritual high that invigorated and vitalized your life.

Affirmation is the community's applause. Think what would happen in your home, in your business, in your community, and yes in your church if affirmation was set loose! God made us dreaming, visioning creatures. Show me a person who has no more dreams, and I will show you someone who needs to plan their funeral. So it was when Peter stood up to preach on the Day of Pentecost. When he searched the index of his mind for a text from the Bible on which to anchor his sermon and interpret the outbreak of the Holy Spirit's power, he chose verses from the prophet Joel. "In the last days it will be, God declares that I will pour out my Spirit upon all flesh, and your sons and your daughters shall prophesy, and your young men shall see visions, and your old men shall dream dreams" (Acts 2:17).

What was Peter saying? In a word, he named the connection between the visioning-dreaming gift of God and the reality of God's Spirit in a community of believers. Affirmation is the community's voice saying, "Because we believe in you, believe for yourself, and embrace all God has for you." Talk about empowering your life! The church at its best shines the spotlight of affirmation on people's dreams, thus enabling them to hear and follow the voice of God.

Finally, shine the light of expectation on the word *accountability*. Wherever you find God's faithful community, you can expect accountability. Accountability, rather than acting as a watchdog on our actions, serves as a trusted safeguard, testing our dreams and visions. Accountability to others, rather than being restrictive, is incredibly freeing. For example, farmers build fences to hold their cattle because they know it is the nature of cattle to roam. Fences protect the cattle from possible danger and enable the farmers to maximize their return on their investments.

Accountability within a faithful community is a trusted fence around human whim. The faithful community, finding allies in both creation and the Bible, is able and available to affirm our dreams and shape our visions. For example, accountability says the dream of marriage to a faithful life-partner is wholesome, enriching, and the foundation of the family. At the same time, persons who want to be in the context of a faithful community and live together outside the covenant of marriage can and should expect the community to call them to God's higher standard of marriage.

The lingering trauma in the church having to do with homosexuality is an accountability issue. The faithful community of acceptance-acknowledgment-affirmation has, does, and will always include homosexuals in the fellowship of believers. What the faithful community does, and what accountability demands, is to say to homosexuals that God's standard for sexual relationships is a heterosexual union in the covenant of marriage. All other unions—homosexual or heterosexual—violate God's ideal. Are homosexuals welcome in the church I serve? Yes. Are homosexuals involved in our church? I would think they are. Does our church condone or, by its silence, accept sexual relationships between same-sex couples? No. Would our church endorse-bless-acknowledge-embrace a homosexual relationship? No. Why? Because we are accountable to God, creation, the Bible, and each other. If God's faithful community is a means by which we hear God's voice, the community must be accountable to God as it has known God in Jesus Christ.

One more word about homosexuality. The church, particularly conservatives within the church, has been accused of rejecting homosexuals, encouraging homophobia, and locking homosexuals out of the fellowship of believers. I find such sweeping accusations unprincipled. The fact is, persons of more liberal persuasion in the church along with conservatives welcome alcoholics, but we do not embrace alcoholism as a normative lifestyle. Believers accept-acknowledge-affirm drug users, spouse abusers, pimps, prostitutes, and embezzlers without condoning their behavior. The entire gospel of Christ begins with grace but results in a changed life. The same relational standards apply to the homosexual and homosexuality. The person is accepted. The unhealthy and unnatural behavior is rejected.

If the church is to function as the faithful community to persons seeking to hear and follow God's voice, the community must be faithful to their Lord. Such is the demand placed upon us and the demand we accept as accountable followers of Christ.

What Happens?

When we walk through the doors of a church or sit down with a group of believers, what happens in the context of community that opens our very beings to hear the voice of God? First, we discover faithful *partners*. Too many among the human family view others as life competitors, not life partners. The Christian faith says we discover meaningful life when we suddenly, miraculously experience God and others as partners.

Look again at your life. How many broken relationships have you lived through because you based them upon the myth of scarcity rather than the reality of abundance? A friendship was growing beautifully until "she" moved to town. And, because you believed there was only so much friendship raw material, "she" stole your friend, and you lost. How many petty little quarrels have divided churches because one "group" tried to control the minister or two families were believed to "run the church"? These behaviors and many more short-circuit our ability to experience the presence and voice of God.

On the other hand, seeing others as partners frees us to listen, to enjoy, to appreciate, to value the gifts we offer to others and those they give in return. Don't be deceived. When the church is the faithful community of worship and witness, there is no shortage of acceptance, acknowledgment, affirmation, and accountability. In fact, the more we give of ourselves to others, the more we have to give. The more we listen to others—their joys, sorrows, fears, questions—the more we open our lives to hear the voice of God. Remember, when you enter a faithful community of believers, you are among partners whose journey is your journey, whose Christ is your Christ, whose love is your love. The word is partners.

Second, we meet authentic, believable *persons*. God's faithful community is not a collection of names, a list of numbers, a gene pool of diversity, or a hodgepodge of opinions. The faithful community is the company of persons like yourself who have been embraced as persons by the person of Jesus Christ. It grieves me to hear church members speak of other members as "they." "They're running the church." "I'll decide whether or not I'll participate in the stewardship campaign when *they*—whoever that is—decide what we're going to do about the soup kitchen." The sentences go on *ad nauseam*. The church may be an institution, but the body of Christ—the faithful community of believers, the spiritual reality having Christ as their Lord and grace as their message—is filled with real, feeling, believing, praying, loving persons.

When you meet up with a faithful community of persons, you find yourself being transformed into a more loving, giving, caring person. You pray with persons like yourself whose children are pursuing the god of success and ignoring the God of love. You hear each other read from the Bible and meet persons such as David who knew great temptation and failure, Ruth who knew unusual loyalty and devotion, and Peter who could be courageous one minute and cowardly the next. God speaks to us as persons through persons. This is the central message of the New Testament. God became a person—a real human being—who lived among us and died for us.

Finally, we find our lives claimed by life-changing *promises*. Within God's faithful community, our lives, lived with partners who are persons, are changed by promises we receive that transform us and make our lives a promise to others. As we participate in a faithful community, we embrace the promises of God that tell us we are God's children living in God's world, embraced by God's love in Christ.

In that transforming relationship we become to others the promise we believe. The faithful community that began as an external grouping of persons now becomes the community of faith to which we belong. Persons we first met as strangers are now addressed as "brother" and "sister." We look around and discover others drifting into the community who, like ourselves, are seeking to hear and follow the voice of God, and we accept them as fellow travelers.

When my daughter was younger, she learned a song with a catchy tune and cute lyrics.

> I am a promise, I am a possibility,
> I am a promise, with a capital "P,"
> I am a great big bundle of potentiality.

I can still see her dancing around the house as she sang that song. Like all children, Lindsey is maturing into the promise she has believed and the promises she is believing. So it is with all who seek partnership with persons in a faithful community. They discover the voice of God in Jesus Christ as experienced in the dynamic community of persons we call brother and sister. This faithful community is the promise of God, the body of Christ, the fellowship of the forgiven, the communion of saints, the family of faith, the church.

Notes

[1]*The Book of Common Prayer* (The Seabury Press, 1979) 430.

[2]A powerful exposition of the Model Prayer as it speaks to prayer's many dimensions and expressions is Kenneth Leech's *True Prayer: An Introduction to Christian Spirituality* (London: Sheldon Press, 1980).

[3]*Emmanuel: Encountering Jesus as Lord* (Cambridge: Cowley Publications, 1992) 9. Herbert O'Discoll's new book *Conversations in Time* explores this very idea.

Chapter 5
THE EMPOWERING DRAMA

The theater holds a certain enchantment for me. A pianist since childhood, I enjoy many forms and styles of music from serious to contemporary. Since my teenage years I've had a warm place in my artistic psyche for Broadway musicals. In high school I was the beneficiary of an unusually gifted chorus teacher who involved his students in a variety of performance media. More gifted at the keyboard than the bass section, Mr. Storm tapped me to accompany the concert choir and the smaller ensemble he named "The Phoenix Singers." Like the mythical Egyptian phoenix, this ensemble of high school students would rise from the ashes of summer vacation to sing and perform all over the greater Miami area. Forgive my bravura, but we were good.

Each year Mr. Storm had us raise money by selling everything from donuts to Christmas candles for one grand purpose. We put together, under his demanding and wise tutelage, a spring musical. I'm talking Broadway—*Carnival*, *South Pacific*, *Camelot*, *Oklahoma*, *Brigadoon*. Miami Springs Senior High School didn't have a championship football team during my three years there, but the chorus department was the talk of the town.

As the years have passed, I've thought about what happens on a stage when, after months of rehearsals and weeks of publicity and days and nights of blood-sweat-tears anguish, the curtain rises and a story bathed in beautiful music begins. It's magic! Whether the company is composed of high school students or seasoned New York thespians, something magical happens when the curtain rises. On stage, in a school auditorium, or on 42nd Street in New York City, a writer's lines, a composer and lyricist's music, glorious costumes, magnificent sets and props, and prepared actors put it all together for three hours of enchantment. Making all of that happen are people connected to each other by the thinnest of personal threads across a span of years and generations and experience and geography. Yet the wound steel cable of the script and the stage bind them to each other. It's a mystery that makes the magic happen.

Could prayer be like the wonder that takes place on stage? Could prayer be the listening-seeing-experiencing wonder of hearing God speak through all God has made and deemed worthy of communicating God's voice? Up to this point in our journey we've looked, if you please, at the theatrical components through which meaningful listening takes place. Could creation, Word, and community together act as stage, script, and company to communicate God's wonder to our heart of hearts? When our lives are focused on the curtain rising before us, listening hearts can experience God's voice in life-changing wonderful ways.

The final stop in our quest to tune our hearts to the voice of God places us in front of the stage of prayer itself. Reach out your hand and grab a bouquet of metaphors for prayer. Conversation, communion, meditation, presence, wish-list wanting, complaining, weeping, and many more would fill your hand. What about the theater? Could prayer be experiencing the wonderful, colorful, musical voice of God through all God has done in and through God's world, God's Word, and God's people? If so, our response must be nothing less than an entering into that drama by speaking back to God with our lives an applauding affirmation of the story God has thrown up on stage. Yes, prayer is conversation, but prayer is much more. On stage the cast speak lines that echo the deeper longings of the human heart. Because they do, we are drawn into the story. Our response is a changed and changing life by the power of God, a life that has heard God's voice and dares speak God's word.

So it is with prayer. We enter the theater of the holy and find ourselves enthralled by the drama God has written. At times we don't understand what we're seeing. We get angry and, rather than applaud, jeer and hiss. "What kind of person would write a story like that? How could God be so heartless, insensitive, and uncaring?" These are the questions-accusations everyone in the audience asks at some time or another. At times we see on the stage what seems absurd, cruel, confusing, or all three.

But soon, almost unperceptively, the music changes. Violins play a gentler, more soothing melody. The drama moves from tragedy to triumph. Buy a ticket and spend three hours experiencing *Les Miserables*, *Phantom of the Opera*, or *Carousel*, and witness the human spirit dip and soar like notes scribbled on music paper. Prayer—empowering, life-changing prayer—is such a transforming experience at a higher, ultimate level of being. Call prayer conversation and communion, but don't stop there! Prayer is sight-sense-spiritual mystery through which God communicates with us and we with God. Such experience is only possible if we dare enter the theater where God takes creation, Word, and community and weaves them together to reveal God anew to those who watch, wait, and listen.

If prayer is such an empowering drama of sight and word and relationships, how can we discover in this experience God's strength so that our tragic-triumphant lives make sense? In the lines that follow I construct a model for understanding prayer as empowering drama. Come with me and glimpse from God's creation, God's Word, and God's people the mystic, transforming glory God gives to those who choose to see and listen, feel and experience God's drama.

Tourists and Travelers

I enjoy travel. Getting out of town for a few days is the best tonic I know to clear my head, renew my physical being, and refocus my energies on God's will and purpose for my life. Through the years I've been allowed the privilege of traveling to places as diverse as Ecuador, England, and Egypt. The world is a fascinating place, filled with beautiful, fascinating people. When you stand in the ruins of the ancient Egyptian temples at Luxor, you cannot help but gasp. There, human beings collected their creative genius and raised those sanctuaries as a gift to their gods. Then it hits you, the human family has been around for a long, long time. In the words of the Bible, our lives "are a mist that appears for a little while and then vanishes" (Jas 4:14). Other "Aha's!" overwhelm you when you travel. When you gaze at the vast expanse that is Canterbury Cathedral, your very being is magnetically pulled upward. You cannot help but say, "O Lord, our Sovereign, how majestic is your name in all the earth!" (Ps 8:1). Travel expands your being and broadens your appreciation for the genius of humanity and the inspiring glory of God.

Put all the people in one room who will pack suitcases this year and go someplace near or far to see and experience other places, and you'll divide that mass of humanity into two groups. One group will be the tourists; the other the travelers. People taking pleasure trips to exotic-historic-beautiful places around Planet Earth neatly divide themselves into these two groups. Which group claims you?

Tourists are in a hurry. They want to see all they can see, do all they can do, and buy as much as they can buy for as little money as possible. Simply put, tourists want to "have it all." Tourists brag about "seeing London" from the top of a double-decker bus. "There's the Tower on your left . . . two blocks is St. Paul's on your right. Yes, that's Buckingham Place. Now look over there; that's Big Ben and Westminster." Tourists are equipped with swivel-heads able to turn in circles like barn owls. Tourists love shopping. Snapshots proliferate like rabbits. Ditty bags contain lots of extra film—don't want to miss a thing—and finger foods comprise a lunch menu for quick eating.

I know tourists. At times I've been and probably will again be one. Growing up in south Florida, "the season" stretched from January to Easter. The snowbirds came south, the racetracks bulged with two-dollar patrons, and traffic was impossible. Tourists move in, soak up whatever they came to "see," and go home. Not all who take trips, however, are tourists.

Travelers have another agenda. Travelers have time. Mind you, travelers are managing the same two-week vacation as tourists; they're just not as frantic about doing everything, seeing everything, and being everywhere. Travelers plan a four-day stay in London: a full day—that won't be enough—at the British Museum; a day for Westminster, Parliament, and Churchill's War Rooms; a day at the Tate Gallery and Madam Tousaud's; and a day meandering through Soho and the shops. Travelers know London theater. They plan their nights and carefully select the shows they want to see. Travelers have time for Evensong at Westminster Abbey (every afternoon around 5:00 for the past 1,000 years!).

Travelers don't mind walking. In fact, walking is preferred; you can rub shoulders with the locals. Travelers eat at the pubs and cafes, and look for side-street bakeries. In a word, travelers linger. I know about travelers; there's one fighting to be born inside this tourist body. Travelers don't see as much, but they experience much more.

So it is with prayer. Tourists see the empowering drama of prayer as a skit. Let's get it over with and get on with the real world. How many meals have been launched with touristy prayers? "Quick! Say a 'brief' word of prayer, so we can devour the food, throw whatever dishes we used in the dishwasher, scatter to the four corners of the house, and continue our lonely tourist existence." "Quick! Start the meeting with a pop-gun prayer, so we can get our hands on the real business of the church."[1] "Quick! Pray over our wedding, and let's get it over with so we can get to the reception and make our way to the delicious delights of the honeymoon." Quick! Quick! Pray!

Travelers, however, find prayer to be another reality altogether. "Prayer." Same word—same London, same Rome, same Jerusalem, same Grand Canyon—only powerfully different. For travelers, prayer is a lingering, longing, meandering, sensing journey with God. Travelers see prayer as an evening's musical you don't want to end. Skits may be nice for parties, but travelers insist that an orchestra, staging, costumes, seasoned actors, and black-tie define the ultimate theater experience. Travelers take time, knowing God's drama of love and passion, tragedy and triumph, heroes and villains, anguish and joy is not some two-bit charade put on by street jesters.

Perhaps you've found prayer to be a nonsense exercise. "I don't have time to pray," "What difference does it make?" and "My prayers don't go any higher than the ceiling" are sentences voicing your past journeys into prayer. Perhaps the ceilings are low, time is oppressive, and the involvement is not meaningful because you've rushed headlong into the presence of holiness thinking you could grasp the mystery of God in one sweeping moment.

Slow down. Prayer's depth, like the wonders of the Grand Canyon, cannot be measured in seconds. The lasting memories travelers make are memories wanting an encore. There, on the stage, the entire drama of right and wrong, faithfulness and forgiveness, is thrown up before your eyes. The lights, the music, the acting, the staging draw you into its story with magnetic power. Suddenly it hits you! "I'm there, somewhere in that story." So it is with prayer. Travel with God through creation, God's Word, God's people and find yourself entering into prayer at a depth previously unknown.

The listening heart hears best when touristic folly is left home with the kenneled pets. Linger, look, experience, wonder, and enter into the empowering drama of prayer. Stop long enough to celebrate God's created world in which you live and, like those who've gone before you, soak in the majesty of God that breaks out every morning and lasts through the day. Pick up the Bible and read with lingering wonder the tragedy and triumph of men and women who, in the depths of their own humanity, were met by God and gasped. Travel for days and weeks (could I say a lifetime?) with God's faithful community of believers and find their stories woven into yours and together, both yours and theirs, woven into the larger drama of God's grace and judgment, mercy and love. It's all there for those willing to leave their tourist past and journey as travelers listening for God's winsome voice.

Doodlers and Artists

I'm bad about doodling on any scrap of paper in front of me. It's a nervous twitch you may be guilty of as well. Most of my doodling is geometric: triangles, lines, squares, circles. Okay, I'm creatively challenged when it comes to the visual arts. Somewhere inside of me is an artist, but time and other interests have submerged the artist allowing the musician-preacher to surface.

My son Justin, unlike his doodling dad, is an artist. He's good. At sixteen, Justin has a God-given ability to put on paper pictures swirling in his imagination. Watching Justin work has led me to a fundamental decision about artists. Artists refuse to stop, to let the particular piece they're working on alone, until it's exactly like the picture they've imagined in their minds. Doodlers don't care. Hey, when I stop drawing lines and circles on an old envelope, I trash it! Artists wouldn't think of doing that with a finished work.

I'm told the world's great artists from Leonardo de Vinci to Picasso were doodlers. The difference is, a Picasso "doodle" is a collector's item (Pablo saved them!). My doodles are collected in a wad and tossed. When it comes to the visual arts, the line is pretty neatly drawn between doodlers and artists.

Prayer's empowering drama is much the same way. As we experience God's creation, read God's Word, and share life with God's people, the temptation to doodle is almost irresistible. That is, we "take in" this three-dimensional communication from God and too easily doodle our reaction to it. There is another response. Taking the time, we could choose to paint on the canvas of our lives the masterpiece God would have us create from listening to God's voice. We could, were it not for overstimulation. The empowering drama can at times overpower us, overwhelm us, overcommunicate God's voice. The result is, we shut down our higher, more artistic selves and scratch out some shallow lines and circles quickly tossed in the wastebasket of frustrated memory.

The temptation to doodle is real. How many times have you found yourself overcome by some twist of inexplicable reality? A cancer diagnosis, a tornado, divorce papers, a slammed door—and doodled off these words: "O God, what am I going to *do* [doodle]?" In moments like that, everything within us wants to fall back on the more angular, rational side of our spiritual selves and draw lines and circles around whatever has happened. We think, "If I can isolate this *thing* from the rest of my life, I can go on." Professionals call this exercise "denial." But doodling life's tragedies into isolation from life's larger drama quickly distorts and maims our lives and robs our future of God's masterpiece. God wants to create in us and with us that which is beautiful if we would stop doodling long enough to listen with our hearts and hear God's artistic voice.

Revisit the doodling temptation for a moment. There, on the slate in front of you is a set of circumstances not of your choosing. At that very moment you begin groping for your pencil and an old envelope, frantically wanting to doodle it off the stage. Tempted with denial, you believe passionately that if you can isolate the "thing," make believe it is not real, and get on with your so-called life, dissonance and ambiguity will disappear. What if, in that moment, you decided to set up an easel, take out your brushes, open your watercolors, and begin to blend that "thing" into the larger canvas of your own relationship with God? What if, in those moments, you tuned in to God's inspiration—God's speaking to you—and heard God say, "The cancer is not the enemy. Take courage and find ways to blend it into your life so those who see the masterpiece you are painting will know that a real, feeling, believing human being created this work to the greater glory of God"?

Artists do not rest until the work in front of them looks like the work inside them. Inside you, placed there by the creative brush strokes of God, is an artist. The drama through which God speaks to your heart is there on stage and will always be there. Artists know how to take what is "there" and immortalize it. Do you see it? The listening heart is also the creating heart; blending the raw material of earth, inspired by the creative genius of God, guided by the caring community of faith, until the masterpiece stands before Jesus in that gallery where all God's artists display the work God empowered them to create.

How do you respond visually, creatively, intentionally to the empowering drama of God? Don't be embarrassed or ashamed if at times you can't help doodling a few lines around whatever has offended your higher vision of the way life ought to be. But don't stop there. Lay your doodling down. Get out your paintbrushes. Who knows what masterpiece you will create.

Notes and Music

Our journey is not complete without a stop in the land of music. Musicians and playwrights have had an enduring relationship through the centuries. No one would call them musicals, but Shakespeare's plays had, in fact, incidental music written for them. Prior to the opening of the curtain and between scenes, chamber music—a couple of recorders, an oboe, a flute—would offer some "mood" music for the moment. Drama and music have been and still are companions in the theater.

It's hard to put your finger on it, but anyone can tell the difference between Frank Sinatra and someone dragged on stage in a karioke bar, given a mike, and asked to sing "Strangers in the Night." Something in our ears, our minds, our very beings knows the difference between an amateur and a professional singer. The same is true for pianists, organists, flutists, guitarists, and so forth. When the lights are brought down and the Phantom of the Opera sings "The Music of the Night," goose-bumps break out all over me. The same reaction doesn't happen when I sing that song! Why? I call the distinction the difference between reading notes and making music.

I began taking piano lessons at six years of age. I took lessons from various teachers for seven years. Though I still do not understand it, God gave me a gift to play the piano. At age twelve I had almost learned George Gershwin's "Rhapsody in Blue" (the whole thing!). Just remembering the work I put into learning that piece makes me break out in a sweat even now. Somewhere in that magnificent piece of American art, I started banging the keys of the piano in absolute frustration. In that moment of collected anxiety, I remember being unable to translate the notes on the page to the keys on the piano. I knew how to read the notes, I knew where the notes were on the keyboard, but the connection wasn't happening.

I remember praying, "God, I know where the notes on that page are on this keyboard. Help me, free me, to go beyond playing the notes there on the page to making music with my hands." This was no sudden conversion, but gradually over the next several weeks, I began to discover a new freedom in my playing. Not one up to that point in my musical training to "play by ear" (hearing a tune and immediately picking it out on the keyboard), I began experimenting with improvisation, arranging, and composing. Suddenly—a few weeks in a lifetime is quite sudden; when measured against the backdrop of eternity, a few weeks isn't even a blink!—notes became music, and a new dimension of my musical development began that I still enjoy and celebrate today.

This note-music distinction can be discerned by seasoned concert goers. Serious musicians whose names are in lights—Zubin Mehta, Jesse Norman, Luciano Pavarotti, and others—command high fees and play to sold-out audiences because their musical genius peeks out from around the notes and between the phrases and above the orchestra. Watch and hear and experience Jesse Norman sing a Verdi aria or "Amazing Grace," and you will be held in rapture by the wonder of her interpretation of the notes. Jesse Norman does much more than sing notes; she makes music.

So it is in our experience of prayer. When God's empowering drama of world, Word, and people come together before our eyes, we too have a choice to make. Will we spend our lives reading the program notes given to us by some usher at the door? Or, will we enter into and experience the empowering drama and, in so doing, choose to make our own music with and in response to the life-experience we receive from God's world, Word, and people? Everyone is in the theater. The majority will see the very drama you will see. Only those who hunger for enduring music will find their lives entering into the theater and being transformed by its power and majesty.

People who live by notes have approved lists of writers, theologians, musicians, poets, and preachers. Anyone not on the list is suspect. I remember being in a Christian bookstore a few years ago with my family. We wanted to purchase an Amy Grant tape. Unable to find "Amy" anywhere, my wife asked the clerk and was quickly told, "We don't stock Amy Grant anymore. You know, she's gone secular." Ugh! That's note-reading. According to the clerk, Amy's not okay anymore because she's sold a couple million copies of a pop song. Baloney!

We're talking here about the prerogative of Almighty God to communicate God's voice through all kinds of media. Are we listening? Some of the most profound spiritual moments I've had in my life have been in a theater. I loved Andrew Lloyd-Weber's *Starlight Express*. That entire musical, performed on roller skates in a theater alive with lights and moveable staging, literally preaches the gospel. There, on a London stage, I witnessed grace, forgiveness, acceptance, faith, and perseverance. God speaks to those who are listening.

Film is another vehicle through which I often hear the voice of God. When Steven Spielberg's masterpiece *Schindler's List* came out, our entire family went to see it. Yes, my children are young teenagers, but we prepared them for it and told them that seeing this film was part of their maturing experience. I sat weeping uncontrollably through the final thirty minutes of that film. There, in black and white, directed by a less-than-religious Jew, was the gospel of transformation and grace. Did you see it? At the end of the movie the worldly, greedy, self-centered Oskar Schindler crosses himself, preaching a conversion he experienced in the midst of history's darkest hour.

So it is for all of us who dare break away from the notes we've been given to read as if those notes were the only avenues of truth on the planet. No, I'm not advocating doing away with the Bible, the creed, the Ten Commandments, or common sense. No, I'm not suggesting "anything goes." What I am advocating is an openness to the music being played all around us. God is speaking from the stage of reality in more than one voice, through more than one set of theological positions, even through more than the Christian community.

I conclude this chapter on the empowering drama with a story from my past. Several years ago—has it been a dozen now?—I was visiting my parents in Marietta, Georgia. At the time my sister and her family were living four doors down from Mom and Dad. Jan (my sister) had purchased an older grand piano and was having it restored. As it so happened, the piano technician was putting the piano back together the afternoon of my visit. Jan said, "You ought to go down and meet this guy. He is a concert tuner who restores calliopes and nickelodeons for fun. Quite interesting to talk to." So I did.

I walked into Jan's family room, and there the piano tuner-technician was putting her grand back together, getting it ready to be tuned. As we talked, I asked him about his work, his hobby of restoring old instruments, and the various people he'd tuned for through the years. He told me he had tuned for one of America's better known pop singers who he described as "obnoxious and impossible to please." After a few minutes, I asked him this question. "Who was the most memorable person for whom you've tuned a piano?" At that moment, his eyes lit up, his facial expression changed, and I knew I was about to hear something very special.

"The most interesting person I've tuned a piano for," he said, "was the late Artur Rubenstein." For those who have forgotten, Artur Rubenstein, who was still playing recitals into his ninth decade of life, will probably be remembered as the twentieth century's greatest pianist. He continued. "On the morning preceding his recital, I came to the theater to tune the piano. About the time I unpacked my tools and had the piano prepared for tuning, I heard footsteps on the stage behind me. I turned around and saw Mr. Rubenstein walking towards me.

"He came up behind me, placed his left hand on my shoulder. After a few moments of small talk, I looked into those eyes that are immortal and asked, 'Mr. Rubenstein, how would you like me to tune the piano?' He said, 'Son, you just get it close. I'll do the rest.' "

Isn't that all God asks of us? In our quest for spiritual maturity, listening for the voice of God requires us to simply get it close, knowing

God will do the rest. If we would dare enter the theater where God speaks and experience with wide-eyed wonder God's creation-Bible-community drama and through it all, choose to be spiritual travelers, artists, and musicians, who knows what God would say to us?

Petty theological differences that have long divided churches and denominations might be finally named for what they are: trivial street fights over nonessential issues. Perhaps our anger at God for not being more like us—more reasonable, predictable, logical—might be transformed into worship and awe at God's God-ness. Perhaps prayer might become a dramatic, lights-costumes-music-plot, transforming experience of being with God that it's never been before. Prayer might move from words to wonder, from memorized lines to memorable living, from one-way speeches to multifaceted, glorious relationship.

Who knows, but that tuning our hearts to God's heart might so transform our days and our nights, our dreams and our nightmares, our tragedies and our triumphs, that life might become the full and meaningful journey Jesus said he came to make it. "I came that [you] may have life, and have it abundantly" (John 10:10). If prayer is not the experience by which we come to know that full and meaningful life, I don't know what is.

I invite you now to turn the page and continue the journey as we consider four of God's many responses to our prayers. Listen carefully and ask yourself if God is not speaking even now to your listening heart.

Notes

[1]I am indebted to Eugene Peterson, *Working the Angles: The Shape of Pastoral Integrity* (Grand Rapids: Wm. B. Eerdmans Publishing Co., 1987) 46-47, for this provocative insight into hurried prayer.

Chapter 6

WHAT PART OF "NO" DO YOU NOT UNDERSTAND?

Our three children had a fairly routine first two years of life. But as any parent knows, there comes a time around a child's second birthday when he or she delights in saying "No." Should we be surprised? During her second twelve months of life—now walking, exploring, toddling—we've said "No, no!" to almost anything she's touched. Electrical sockets have especially fascinated her and terrified us. All children learn "No" from their parents. It's one lesson we teach well.

Throughout our lives we struggle with the "No's" to our requests. This is particularly true in our relationships within our family. No one who expects a "Yes" handles "No" without difficulty. So it is with prayer and our relationship to God. There comes a point in this conversation, this dialogue we have with God, where we find ourselves lost and confused. This confusion has to do with the times we pray and those many times we listen, and the answer we receive from God is "No."

"No" often throws us into spiritual confusion. We ask ourselves, "Did God hear me?" Or, "Perhaps God didn't understand me." Or even, "Perhaps if I raised my voice or rephrased the question, I would get the answer I want." We are confused.

Unresolved, this spiritual confusion can lead to anger. We look up to heaven and ask, "Why not? Why didn't you give me the answer I wanted?" Our anger is God-focused. We are frustrated. Many feelings well up within us we don't know how to handle. Unresolved anger often leads to deal-making with God. We reason, "Maybe if I prayed more." "Maybe if I prayed more fervently." "Maybe if I prayed more often." "Maybe if I prayed more sincerely." "Maybe if I went to church Sunday night or started attending prayer meeting." "Maybe if I were nice to my boss." The deals, negotiated in confusion, only multiply.

If we took the time to write out our responses to God's "No," we might see how childish and immature we can be in our relationship with God. For example, I've heard people say that when God didn't give them what they wanted, they planned to start tithing. "Yes, that's the reason I'm not getting the answer I want. I'm holding out on God. So, I'll start tithing, and God will give me what I want."

Call it deal-making. The formula is predictable. "If I do this, God will do that." But what do we do when we make the deal, having raised our voice and rephrased the request and prayed more sincerely (whatever that means), and the answer is still "No"?

Perhaps you've seen the bumper sticker. I normally find it on a van full of children driven by a hurried parent. It reads, "What part of 'No' do you not understand?" In your relationship with God, as you commune with God in prayer, what part of "No" do you not understand? What do we do when God says "No?"

We have a partner in our journey. His name is Paul. Paul had a crisis in his life he called "a thorn . . . in my flesh, a messenger of Satan to torment me" (2 Cor 12:7). Just what was it, this thorn Paul asked God to remove? Early Christian luminaries such as Tertullian, Jerome, and Pelagius suggested the "thorn" was a "pain in the ear or head." John Chrysostom, the golden-throated orator of Constantinople, argued "Paul's thorn was his opponents in the church." Many others through the centuries—mostly in parish situations—have jumped on the John Chrysostom bandwagon and said, "Yes, that was the thorn." Paul asked the Lord to "remove" those people opposing him. "Take them away," he prayed.

Others have been more specific. Lightfoot called the thorn "epilepsy." Ramsey interpreted it as "a form of recurring malarial fever." Many others have identified Paul's thorn as glaucoma. Regardless of what "it" was, Paul said, "Three times I appealed to the Lord about this, that it would leave me" (v. 8). Paul fervently, faithfully prayed three times, "Take it away," and God's answer was, "No."

Perhaps we could understand God's "No" to a Baptist preacher or a "No" to some ordinary mortal Christian, but this was "No" to the apostle Paul. This was a "No" to the great missionary of the first century. This was a "No" to the person who wrote half of the New Testament. This wasn't anybody. This was Paul. God said, "No, Paul. Not you, not this, not now, no."

What part of "No" do we not understand? What do we do when we faithfully listen and God says "No"?

Listen with your heart; Paul's journey can be ours. First, accept the truth that God's "No" to your request is not a "No" to you. Every parent knows the agony of teaching a child this important lesson. "No" to a child's demands is not saying "No" to the child. In fact, a parental "No" to a child's request is often an emphatic "Yes" to the child. For the parent to say "No" to the three-year-old who is about to drink poison is a "Yes" to the child.

As children get older, the "No's" take on greater significance. "Dad, can I go to Jeremy's house Saturday night?" "Will his parents be there?" asks the concerned father. "I'm not sure." "Will there be alcohol in the home?" With head down, the child shrugs his shoulders. Lovingly, but firmly, the father says, "No, son, you can't go to Jeremy's Saturday night."

The "No" to the request is not a "No" to the person. Quite the contrary. The "No" to the request is an emphatic, unequivocal, faithful, loving "Yes" to the child. Paul said as much to the Corinthians:

> As surely as God is faithful, our word to you has not been "Yes and No." For the Son of God, Jesus Christ, who we proclaimed among you, Silvanus and Timothy and I, was not "Yes and No"; but in him it is always "Yes." For in him every one of God's promises is a "Yes." For this reason it is through him that we say the "Amen," to the glory of God (1 Cor 1:18-20).

Paul delighted in saying that God has irrevocably, unforgettably spoken a "Yes" to every human being in Jesus Christ. We may hear "No" to a request, but God has said "Yes" to us. How is it that we can get lost and not remember that?

For one thing, forgetfulness is part of the human package. We confuse "Yes" with "No" from individuals. We mistakenly think the "No" or the "Yes" is somehow a rejection or affirmation of us. With God, God's "No" to our request is not a "No" to us. I'm told that in

Bulgaria, when you nod it means "No," and when you shake your head it means "Yes." This is very confusing if you are traveling in Bulgaria. Most travelers probably don't know any Bulgarian. When people ask you a question that, of course, you need translating, and you want to answer affirmatively, you instinctively nod your head. But that means "No" in Bulgaria.

Now friends, God is not a Bulgarian. Neither is God an American. We must remember God's "No" to our request is always spoken nodding to us. You may hear God saying "No," but God's nod is an irrevocable affirmation of you. God's "No" to your request is not a "No" to you.[1]

There is something else here. Not only is God's "No" to your request not a "No" to you, but God's "No" to your request is not a "No" to grace. Paul said, "Three times I pleaded with the Lord." The verb in the original Greek language is *parakaleo*. Translated "pleaded," it can also mean "begged" or even "demanded." "Three times I demanded from the Lord—I begged the Lord—take this thorn away." But God's answer was, "No, my grace is sufficient for you." God said grace is enough. "No" to our request is not a "No" to grace.

With God, grace is always "Yes." Yet our praying and listening can be polluted by spiritual forgetfulness. All of us know this is so. We cut our teeth on this kind of theology. It's common and popular—it's who we are—but it's dead wrong. This kind of theology says, "God responds affirmatively when I'm good, but negatively when I'm bad." This, of course, is our own self-evaluation. When the answer is "No," we instinctively ask, "What did I do or fail to do that God would not grant my request?" Or, "Where did I mess up?" Because the answer is "No," we assume and say under our breath, "I've done something wrong, or God would answer my prayers and give me what I want." Can we hear the child within refusing to grow up?

The opposite is equally true when we sense God's answer to our prayers is "Yes." We say, "Hey, God's in His heaven; all is right with the world. I got the raise, the promotion. Life's wonderful. Isn't God good. He must really love me." When in fact, because of grace, God loves us no less when we sin than God loves us when we are faithful. Failure-sin-tragedy on the one hand and happiness-success-joy on the other are not wired to grace. Yet, no sooner than we begin to interpret life as if they are, the forgetful fog of spiritual amnesia dulls our senses to authentic grace.

I don't know anybody who doesn't love *The Sound of Music.* When Richard Rodgers and Oscar Hammerstein gave us that musical, they gave us an enduring gift. When Robert Wise put it on the big screen, we fell in love forever with Julie Andrews and Christopher Plummer (mostly with Julie Andrews). Every parent knows from beginning to end both the music and the story of *The Sound of Music.* Some of you are *Sound of Music* junkies. You've rented the film and watched it dozens of times. I know you folks; I'm the same way. One of the first films we rented for our children was *The Sound of Music.* We love the songs, especially Oscar Hammerstein's wonderful way with words. "The hills are alive with the sound of music," "How Do You Solve a Problem Like Maria?" "I've Got Confidence in Confidence Alone." And when you're really low, just like Maria, you want somebody to come into your life and sing, "Climb Every Mountain," just like the Reverend Mother did looking out over the Alps.

There is one scene in *The Sound of Music* that always brings out the hankies. You get ready for it, because you have seen the movie so many times. You know the scene is coming, so you reach in your pocket and get your hankie or box of tissues ready. It's that wonderful scene when Maria comes back from the convent. The wealthy Baroness and Captain Von Trapp are out on the porch, and Maria goes off into the woods of the estate all alone.

The Captain looks at the Baroness and says, "It's not going to work"—you're getting your hankie ready—"You know, and I know there's no future to this. It's hard to marry someone when you're in love with someone else." The Baroness replies, "I know. But there is somebody out there (Maria) who's not going to make a very good nun."

In the next scene the Captain goes out into the forest and, sure enough, there is Maria, and they have this teenage conversation.

"Well, what are you doing here?" And in the next few moments, Maria is no longer a governess, and the Captain becomes Georg. They look deeply into each other's soul, and love drowns them and us in overwhelming emotion. Now we're blotting tears dribbling down our cheeks. The violins start playing, and Maria and Georg sing that unforgettable duet.

> I must have had a wicked childhood,
> I must have had a miserable youth,
> But somewhere in my wicked, miserable past,
> There must have been a moment of truth.
> For here you are, standing there, loving me;
> Whether or not you should.
> So somewhere in my youth or childhood,
> I must have done something good.

Now, come the lines with which we most identify:

> Nothing comes from nothing,
> Nothing ever could.
> So somewhere in my youth or childhood,
> I must have done something good.

We're all sniffling, and the hankies are wiping, and we are drawn into Maria and Georg's story like never before, all the while saying, "What a wonderful song. Look at what can happen in your life if there's just the smallest bit of good there." I love that magical moment in the film—I cry every time. The song is wonderful, but it is not a song about grace. The song says, "Nothing comes from nothing, nothing ever could, so somewhere in my youth or childhood, I must have done something good." And we say, "Yes! Yes!" Because that's the way we interpret reality. The good in our lives is the result of the good we do.[2]

But the Bible says, "No!" God is not passing out favors because we are good, nor is God withholding favors because we are bad. God extravagantly pours grace into our lives, not because of any merit we have earned, but solely because God is the One who gives unmerited favor to us, God's human creation. Ours is a maddening confusion. We think God's "No" to our request is a shutting off of God's grace. Nothing could be further from the truth. Don't miss it.

God's "No" to your request is not a "No" to grace. For grace, amazing full and free, is given by a loving God through Jesus Christ to all without qualification, merit, or favoritism.

There is nothing we could do in our childhood, youth, or adulthood that would move or motivate God to love us less or give us more in Christ and in grace than God is giving us now. God's "No" to our request is not a "No" to us, and God's "No" to our request is never a "No" to grace.

There is one more thing. God's "No" to our request is a "Yes" to growth. God's "No" is an invitation to grow. When God says "No" to our request, God is inviting us to grow as human beings, as believers, in fellowship and relationship with God. Paul wrote, "I will boast all the more gladly of my weaknesses, so that the power of Christ may dwell in me. . . . for whenever I am weak, then I am strong" (vv. 9-10). God's "No" is an invitation to grow.

The mystery of human growth is a phenomenon all of us witness in our lives, particularly in the lives of children. Children grow up. Some of you parents don't believe that right now. You think you are going to be in diapers until you die. No! As a rule, children do not go to kindergarten in diapers. Children do grow up. Albeit, there are persons who are physically and/or mentally challenged who have difficulty working through the maturation process. But a human being, with full functioning genes and chromosomes, is on automatic pilot. Physically, we grow automatically. You have to feed the physical body, rest it, put water in it, and take care of it. Do that, and a body will grow from infancy to adulthood. That happens automatically because of the way we're genetically wired.

Unlike physical growth, spiritual growth does not happen automatically. We don't mature spiritually and emotionally in the same way we do physically. If you grow spiritually and emotionally, you grow because you choose to grow. That's why there are persons in their sixties and seventies and even eighties who have lived decades physically but have never matured spiritually and emotionally. They are still adolescents. They behave in adolescent ways, playing games with people, refusing to grow up, and inflicting great anguish and pain on themselves and others.

Spiritual and emotional growth is always a choice. In 2 Corinthians, Paul is convinced God's "No" to what we want contains God's invitation to us to grow as persons. Don't waste your suffering. Don't toss your pain in the wastebasket of regret. Rather, let your pain, your disappointments, and even your failures be the fuel God uses to shape your spiritual growth. Such courage born of faith will mature you into the full and Christlike person God calls you to become.

In his classic book *Creative Suffering*, Paul Tournier has two powerful sentences about the relationship between suffering, creativity, and growth:

> While suffering may not be creative in itself, we are scarcely ever creative without suffering. As the idea of creativity involves to a greater or less degree those of growth and development, one could also say that it is not suffering which makes a person grow, but that one does not grow without suffering; again, that all deprivation and all suffering are opportunities for creativity.[3]

To become the full, mature person God calls us to be summons creativity and growth to rise from the ashes of suffering and even failure. Responding with creative courage to God's "No" is surely one way we seize our full humanity in Christ.

But what do we do instead? How do we typically, instinctively respond when we hear God's "No?" We sulk, we grit our teeth, and we sit down on the prickly sofa of resignation. We say, "Ain't it awful." God said, "No," and we say, "Forget it, I'm out of here." We forget we have another choice.

On the one hand the choice is to withdraw, to resent, to join the whiners club, and to seek allies for a pious pity party. "I've prayed. I've gone to church. I've given the Lord my tithe. I've . . . I've . . . I've . . ." We gather people around us for a complaining session. And there are many who will join in the complaining. That's one choice.

The other choice is to ask: What am I learning, and how can I grow through this experience? We can spend our lives seeking the counsel and pity and succor of people all around us who are not growing anymore than we are and never move into a deeper, challenging, more enriching relationship with Jesus Christ. We can whine our way to our graves and never grow. Many do.

In his compelling book *The Ragamuffin Gospel*, Brennan Manning writes of his own liberating discovery of God's undeserved, unexpected, surprising grace. He describes in many ways this choice we have between listening only to people and people's opinions or growing intimately into a relationship with Christ. He writes:

> We must never allow the authority of books, institutions, or leaders to replace the authority of *knowing* Jesus Christ personally and directly. When the religious views of others interpose between us and the primary experience of Jesus as the Christ, we become unconvicted and unpersuasive travel agents handing out brochures to places we have never visited.[4]

When the voices we hear and believe are not those informed by God's world, Word, and people, we can, without thinking, become nothing more than puppets, parroting the opinions of people—even well-meaning people—who may not be growing themselves.

Are we listening? When God says "No," what do you do? Revisit God's "No" for a moment and, in so doing, find yourself embraced by God's "Yes"—"Yes" to you, "Yes" to grace, and "Yes" to growth. Go back to that "No." Remember that God's "No" to your request is not a "No" to you. In fact, to your surprise, you may discover in that moment God was wrapping arms of acceptance around you.

I invite you to unclench your fist and unwind your bitterness and find yourself awash in amazing grace you can never earn or deserve. That grace is yours because of Christ and in Christ. I invite you to grow. Let God's "No" be an opportunity to grow. Growing requires choosing. Choose to grow, and you will discover grace and affirmation that's been there all along and, to make it even better, God's strength to be the person God created you to be. Don't let God's "No" to your request turn you away from God's everlasting, eternal "Yes" to you. Keep listening. "No" is but a cipher when spoken in the presence of God's all-embracing "Yes" in Christ.

Father, help me today and everyday to be listening from my heart and in listening to know that even when the answer is not what I want, when the answer from your throne of petition and grace is "No" to my request, that I will have the courage to affirm your "Yes" of me and discover you have already embraced me with your grace. In your arms of acceptance, grant me the courage to choose maturity over immaturity and, in so doing, choose life over death. Open my heart to be ever grateful for grace unexpected and undeserved, choosing to grow into the person you created me to be in Christ. This I pray faithfully in the name of the One who taught us that your love is always "Yes," Amen.

Notes

[1]In James W. Cox, *The Minister's Manual* (San Francisco: Harper SanFrancisco,1992) 318.

[2]Ibid., 311.

[3]Paul Tournier, *Creative Suffering*, trans. Edwin Hudson (London: SCM Press, 1982) 110.

[4]Brennan Manning, *The Ragamuffin Gospel* (Sisters OR: Multnomah Books, 1990) 42.

Chapter 7

IS "YES" GOD'S BEST?

One of my beloved teachers and friends in ministry and life is Dr. Harold Songer, now retired vice-president of The Southern Baptist Theological Seminary in Louisville, Kentucky. Harold takes great delight in telling the story of the time one of his students told him with great happiness, "All my problems are over! When I proposed, she said, 'Yes.' " When the laughter died down, Dr. Songer reminded us all, such a naive interpretation of "Yes" awaits the real world discovered in a real marriage between two real and fragile people.

Why is it that when we hear a "Yes" to our wants, we assume, like the naive student, "all our problems are over"? A more thoughtful response, sobered by life lived in God's chaos-order creation, informed by the Word, and more fully interpreted by the community gives us reason to ask: What does God's "Yes" to our prayers mean?

We have an expression in our arsenal of words that's not very flattering. We call someone who is always trying to please everybody a "Yes man" or a "Yes woman." Obsequious and often shallow, "Yes" people put aside their own selves not in the interest of others, but in an effort to protect themselves. "Yes" people try to please others so they can continue to live in the illusion that "everybody likes me." This, of course, empowers them—living in the illusion—to say, "I like myself."

Calling someone a "Yes man" is not a compliment. To the contrary, the epithet is critical: we see in that individual a person with very little conviction or backbone. Our youth call "Yes" people wimps. We have little respect for "Yes" people.

Yet in our relationship with God, we pray, lifting our requests to God's throne of mercy, wanting God to say "Yes" to our petitions. We make the requests, yearning for God's "Yes." How many times have you reasoned, "*If* God loves me, *if* I'm praying 'in the Spirit,' *if*

I'm cleansed from sin, *if* I pray 'in Jesus' name,' I'll hear God's 'Yes' "? Somewhere inside, we know—don't we?—that in Christ, God has spoken "Yes" to us. Yet we want God to respond with a "Yes" to our petitions; our "give me's" are ever hungry for God's "Yes."

This way of relating to God and interpreting God's relationship to us is risky business. On a more human level, what parent doesn't long for the day when their children move away from being "give me" human beings toward the land of maturity? Children want, need, demand, and insist on their own way. Children never tire of making demands and awaiting the demanded "Yes." On the other hand, adults—mature human beings—are persons who learn that life has another, more rewarding, more fulfilling side. Jesus put it this way: "Whoever wants to save his life will lose it, but whoever loses his life for me will find it" (Matt 16:25).

The listening heart, longing for God's approval, can and often does miss full communion with God because "Yes" is the only answer that will satisfy. The more I've thought about this, the more I am aware that in forty-four years of living and more than twenty years in the ministry, no one has ever said to me in a spirit of confidence and assurance, "God answered my prayers," meaning the answer was "No."

Listen to the conversations about prayer around you. Listen in your Sunday School class or at work when someone says, "God answered my prayer." You assume, don't you, the answer God gave the person talking was "Yes." For most of us, answered prayer means a "Yes" from God. When this reality dawned on me, I began to look at my own prayer vocabulary. To my embarrassment as a Christian and shame as a minister, I came to the place where I had to admit much of my prayer language is punctuated by this idea that God's best answers to prayer are "Yes" answers.

To make matters worse, numbers of books have been written on posturing our prayers in such a way so that God will answer us in the affirmative. One has to ask if such an approach to prayer doesn't suggest God can be conned, manipulated, or pressured. I can remember hearing a preacher not too many years ago declare that if you are cleansed of sin and living in the Spirit, you need not pray "Thy will be done." With cocky bravura, he told the congregation that such "caboose clauses" on our prayers are cop-outs. Real Christians—his voice was rising at this point—know God's will and can ask for and should expect God's answer to agree with their requests. Meaning? God's answer should be and must be "Yes" (when, of course, we remember to include all the right clauses, addendums, and formulas in our prayers).

This way of reasoning could produce books with provocative titles such as: *How to Get a "Yes" from God, Five Steps to Successful Prayer*, or *God's Best Is "Yes."* God deliver us from such shallow, childish theological and spiritual nonsense!

Less we be too self-righteous ourselves, we all listen with itchy ears for someone to tell us of the "Yeses" they have received from God. But alas, with answers in hand, we are no more ready for life than we were before the testimonies began. What are we to do? That's our question, isn't it? When our hearts are listening, what do we do when God does say "Yes" to our prayers? But before we attempt to answer that question, we must think for a moment of some unhealthy responses to God's "Yes." I *do believe* God answers many of our prayers in the affirmative. The issue I ask you to join me in wrestling with has to do with the "What now?" *after* we've heard God's "Yes."

Three Unhealthy Responses

In order to answer the "What now?" with any degree of success, we must first look at a few of the unhealthy responses to God's "Yes." The first of many unhealthy responses to God's "Yes" is *bragging*. In a word, bragging is pride disguised as piety, boasting to others about God's "Yes." With inflated spiritual chests, strutting pietistic peacock feathers, we brag about "The Lord this" and "the Lord that" with deaf ears to the pride oozing out from our self-centered interpretations to answered prayer.

One of the personal-professional challenges I face daily is how to be a minister without broadcasting—either by the way I dress or that ministerial "look"—that I am a minister. Try as I do, every once in a while, in mid-conversation, I'm discovered. "And what do you do?" they ask, knowing the answer. "I'm a minister." Their eyes shout, "I knew it!" Suddenly, without warning, the vocabulary and conversation change. Believe me, there is a segment of the human family—more prominent in the Bible Belt—that delights in cornering ministers with questions and/or "let-me-tell-you-what-God's-done-for-me" testimonials.

When one of these folks finds out I'm a minister, our pleasant conversation about baseball suddenly changes to "The Lord this" and "The Lord that." What's even more strange about this phenomenon is that up to that point in the conversation prior to my being discovered (when I'm simply another person), the one with whom I'm speaking was telling me "I this" and "I that." Are they more believable because "the Lord" has replaced "I" as the source of one's decisions and actions? You tell me. In my judgment, such bragging is raw pride disguised as piety. Bragging about God's "Yes" actually takes the spotlight off of God and puts it on us. We may begin our sentences with "The Lord . . . ," but what we can mean is, "If you were as holy as me, you'd receive a 'Yes' from God, too."

Yet, when God reveals God's "Yes" to our prayers, we want to give God praise. We want to throw the spotlight away from self and on God who delights in giving good gifts to God's children. Even so, thanksgiving for God's blessings and bragging disguised as piety are not the same thing. Thanksgiving flows from a grateful heart; bragging rushes headstrong out of a self-centered ego. Thanksgiving is God-focused; bragging revels in proving how "holy" I am. Thanksgiving invites others to join us in praise; bragging turns others off and away. Be on your guard against yielding to the temptation to brag.

A second unhealthy response to God's "Yes" is what I call *consuming*. That is, we feast on God's "Yes." We find ourselves becoming spiritually obese and fattened by God's "Yes" to our prayers.

A businessman came up to a minister and said, "Last year I made $250,000. But you know pastor, since I made all that money, it has become really difficult for me to tithe; taxes just eat up so much." The minister said to the businessman, "I'm sorry to hear that. I guess I'll have to pray you make less money next year so you can get back to the place where you can tithe."

When we become consumers of God's "Yes," we all too quickly find ourselves hungry for more. Like greedy children, consuming God's "Yes" on ourselves is a very unhealthy way of relating to God. It cheapens God's grace and, worse than that, cheapens our own humanity made in God's image and reborn in Christ.

Materialism may be the most destructive god of this age. Lest I speak of others' battles while remaining safe behind my word processor, let me talk about my fight with materialism. God has indeed blessed me with good health, a loving and giving wife, three intelligent and "neat" children who also are my friends, and a generous and, I'll say it, prosperous church in which to live out my pastoral calling. The church I serve is known for excellence in every aspect of its life. The members are most generous with me as their pastor and with all their ministers and employees. To make matters better, they pay me well. I'm grateful for their faithfulness and generosity.

The temptation I face and you face and most middle- to upper-class American believers face is the temptation to equate directly our "much" with God's "Yes." Let me be even more honest. God endowed me with a good mind and an excellent education and a partner in life whose calling is as certain as my own. God has given me good and lasting and precious gifts. But if I'm not careful, I will consume God's good gifts—material as well as spiritual—on myself. I'll be careful to return to God my tithe, of course; an offering here and there, of course; and think that, having done that, I can do whatever I please with the rest.

Believer beware! Materialism is infecting the contemporary church with the ugly virus of Consumer Christianity. Consumer Christianity reasons that God's "Yes" is our prosperity. And if I return to God something (forget tithing at this point—Americans give less than 2 percent of their income to charitable causes of all kinds, including the church), then I can get on with my life as I please. God's got what God wants; I can manage the rest, thank you!

Caution! Believers who interpret God's "Yes" as something like divine parental permissiveness are living light-years from spiritual maturity. Make no mistake about it, consuming God's good gifts on ourselves, refusing to see God's "Yes" as God's opportunity to bless others, is sin. Perhaps your promotion to CEO of the company, with its stock options and bonuses, is not God saying, "Build a bigger home for yourself" and getting away with it by bragging about the Lord's blessings. Perhaps God's gifts of health, education, opportunity, and financial success are messages from God saying, "Give more of your income away. Pour more of yourself into helping the poor, mentoring one-parent children, and using your influence to convince government to be more humane." I don't know what God would have you do with God's "Yes" to your prayers, but I am convinced God will not let me consume God's blessings as if they were my own.

I'm thinking of several generous people I know in our church who, very quietly but deliberately, are making a difference in the lives of others with the material blessings of God. They've not built a new house, they've not bought an expensive car, and they've not put more "rings on their fingers" and "bangles" on their wrists. Quite the contrary. With unusual humility and generosity, year after year, they give more and more to God's work, believing God has blessed them for one reason: that they might bless others. That's the kind of materialism I want to see in my life; giving the material away to the greater glory of God.

There is a third unhealthy response to God's "Yes." I call it *analyzing* how we got a "Yes" so we can get another one. How did I pray? Was I good this week? Did I go to church? Did I pay my tithe and give an offering? How did I get to "Yes?"

Like the previous two unhealthy responses to God's "Yes," analyzing is rooted in immaturity. Any parent knows how quickly children can "play" one parent against the other or, for that matter, "play" you—the parent—for all you're worth. Children quickly learn to analyze parental response to their cries for help.

If you're a parent, you've had this experience. Your first child cries, and you hold her. Every time the child cries, you pick her up.

Good job! That's what responsible parents do. As the child gets a little older, however, she cries when she's not hungry, not colicky, not needing a diaper change. Your daughter learns—and yes, you taught her—that crying leads to holding. And, come to think about it, who among us doesn't like to be held? The parents are a quick read to a child and, before you can say "spoiled," the child has analyzed the parents and will, if not taught otherwise, get what she wants. Parents beware!

Being the human beings we are, we can and do get into relational ruts with God built upon analyzing God's responses to our prayers and needs. To be human is to be analytical. Even so, analyzing can become a very unhealthy response to God's "Yes." Be on your guard for any and all literature, preachers, teachers, and other well-meaning faith partners who, with engineering precision, can tell you "how to" pray so as to insure from God the answer you want. Analyzing is an imperative and useful tool for attorneys, engineers, Bible scholars, teachers, parents, physicians, and all of us. Analyzing our journey in prayer in order to secure a "Yes" answer from God can be dangerous and even deadly.

Three Maturing Responses

Having named three unhealthy responses we can and do make to God's "Yes"—there are surely more—what is a more appropriate, maturing, empowering way to respond to the perceived "Yes" we receive from God?

There is a wonderful story in the New Testament about a "Yes" God gave to God's people. In Acts 12:1-17, we find a story that reveals to us more of the relational essence of the early church than perhaps any story in the New Testament. This story is so utterly believable. It's played out on two stages simultaneously. On the first stage it displays the wonder and power of God among God's people. On the second stage it witnesses to God's power at work within the transparent humanity of persons in the infant church. When I read this story, I see God and us relating to each other at various levels. This moment in the early church was very stressful. Believers had been arrested including James the brother of John, one of the original four disciples. Not only had James been arrested, but Herod had executed him. As Acts 17 begins, Herod has also arrested Peter. The time? Passover and the Feast of Unleavened Bread.

These were stressful days. To revisit Passover for the church was to bring back all kinds of memories: memories of another trial, of another execution, of other terrors. It was Passover time, and memories of crucified horror were no doubt alive in the young church.

While Peter was in prison, the church was having a prayer meeting. The following day, Herod's agenda included trying and probably executing Peter. If Herod had his way, within a few hours, the church would suffer the loss of its leader. First it was Jesus, then James, and now Peter. This is high drama for a group of believers who had no political clout, no vote, no "PAC," no money, no anything but empty-tomb faith.

While the church was having a prayer meeting in a house, Peter was locked away on death row, chained between two guards. This was the maximum security block otherwise known as Herod's dungeon. For his part, Peter was not biting his nails, pacing the floor—he was chained—or raising the roof shouting. Don't miss it: Peter was asleep in the jail while the church prayed!

Suddenly, an angel told Peter to get up and follow him. To his surprise, the chains fell off, the door opened, and angel-led Peter simply walked out of Herod's maximum security dungeon. Dumbfounded by this experience, Peter thought he was having a dream; a good dream for sure, but a dream nonetheless. The angel and Peter passed the first set of guards, then the second. Eventually, they came to the iron gate that separates imprisonment from freedom, death from life. Together they walked through the open gate. They went a bit further. When Peter looked down to walk over an open manhole, and then looked up, the angel was gone—vanished, kaput!

Realizing this was not a dream, Peter walked quickly to the place where the prayer meeting was being held. He knocked on the door. Nothing. He knocked again—must have been a very verbal prayer meeting. No one could hear the doorknocker. Finally, a servant girl named Rhoda came to the door, recognized Peter, and slammed the door in his face as she ran back upstairs shouting, "It's Peter! It's Peter!"

Peter, not known to be the retiring type, kept knocking. Finally, the prayer meeting crowd opened the door, put a couple dozen hugs around their leader, and took him inside. After telling the whole dumbfounded, amazed, teary-eyed upper room group his story, Luke tells us Peter "left for another place."

That's the story in a nutshell. It's a story about a "Yes" God gave to a person and an entire church. What is God saying through God's Word, in that community and that time, to our lives and our community of faith in this time? Specifically, what do we do when our heart listens and we hear a "Yes" from God? What is the story telling us about how we respond to God's "Yes?"

The first thing I hear the story telling us is that God's "Yes" is often revealed to us as an unexpected *surprise*. God's "Yes" is not an expected "Yes." God's "Yes" may not even be a requested "Yes." God's "Yes" is a surprising "Yes." In fact, notice three surprises in this one story. The first surprise is the surprising prayer. In Acts 12:5, Dr. Luke tells us, "While Peter was kept in prison, the church prayed fervently to God for him." We are not told the content of that prayer. I suspect if we had organized the prayer meeting, if we knew our church leader was in prison, knowing he was going to be executed the next morning, we would have voiced very specific prayers. "Lord, set him free." "Get him out of jail." "Make Herod see the light." Or perhaps we would be praying, "Lord turn those trained soldiers, those bloodthirsty killers, into mild-mannered Barney Fife types."

We would have placed much content in the prayer; directing God, making suggestions, or worse, telling God what and how to do what needed to be done. Don't miss it. Luke says the church was praying for *Peter*, not telling God how to rescue Peter. What do you imagine was the content of those prayers for Peter? Could it be the church was praying that Peter would be true to his Lord regardless of what happened? Could it be that they prayed he would speak boldly his love for Christ? Could it be the believers were praying they would be empowered and the church strengthened regardless of what happened to Peter? I think so.

For us, so comfortable in giving God orders, this is a surprising prayer. We would pray telling God what to do. I suspect they were praying for strength and wisdom and courage as they responded in that moment and in the days to come to the future God had for Peter and the church. What would *they* do in the unknown circumstances that were before them? Praying for deliverance is a good prayer; praying for courage before a future that may not include deliverance is an empowering, maturing prayer (Paul's comment on this in Philippians 1:19-20 is especially helpful). We would be wise to learn the difference between asking God to do something with our circumstances and doing something with us. Deliverance has to do with circumstances; courage has to do with me.

The second surprise was Peter's surprising release. Peter thought he was seeing a vision (v. 9). Peter was chained to the wall. Two chains—guards everywhere—guards inside and outside the jailhouse. All of a sudden, the chains fell off, and Peter was walking out of the prison. Apparently, the soldiers who were assigned to guard him either ignored his escape or had fallen asleep and didn't know he had left. The point is, Peter walked through this whole experience totally dumbfounded. It was a surprising release. Peter did not anticipate a "Yes" to this situation at this moment in his life. Jesus had been crucified around Passover; James was already dead; he would be next. Honesty compels us to face this stark probably in Peter's life, even as he did that night in the long ago.

There is a third surprise: a surprising reunion. You've got to love Rhoda. I recently found myself in hot water over this colorful character in the early church. I blurted out to a Bible study group, "Rhoda was the original dingbat." And somebody said, "My mother is named Rhoda." Another said, "My favorite aunt is Rhoda." I was in trouble. Be that as it may, Rhoda came to the door and saw Peter there. Mind you, Rhoda and the others had been praying for Peter. She was so startled when she opened the door—even though she had been praying for Peter—Rhoda slammed the door in his face! Why did she do that? Here's my take: Rhoda had been in a prayer meeting where believers were praying—don't miss it—not for

Peter's release, but, as I hear it, for Peter to have courage. God's "Yes" for Peter and Rhoda was a complete surprise to both of them.

Back to the story. Rhoda slammed the door in Peter's face, ran back into the crowded upper room, and said, "Peter's here." They said of her the same thing they said of Mary and the other women who saw the risen Christ on Easter morning: "Can't be Peter. Rhoda's crazy" (compare Acts 12:15 with Luke 24:11). Even so, there was a surprising reunion. God's "Yes" to us is often surprising. If you've gotten your list out and you are making all kinds of specific requests, don't be so specific that God cannot surprise you with a "Yes" you never anticipated.

There is something else in this story about God's "Yes." This "something else" is extremely difficult for all of us to hear and to believe and to live: God's "Yes" is *no private blessing*. Peter was released from prison. Set free, Peter did not first go off and do his own thing. First, he went to the church. Notice, not only did he go to the place where the church was, he said, "Tell this to James and to the believers. Then he left and went to another place" (Acts 12:17). Peter didn't do his own thing before bringing God's "Yes" into the community of believers. Do you see it? God's "Yes" is not for private consumption. God's "Yes" is not some private, personal blessing consumed on yourself. Whatever else God's "Yes" may mean, it surely means others are there someplace. "Yes" by definition brings others into worship and praise and gratitude.

This truth may be glimpsed no better than in Paul's letter to the Philippians. Paul was in prison. He was separated by hundreds of miles from people he loved, and yet he wrote back to his Philippian friends with these words:

> For I know that through your prayers and the help of the Spirit of Jesus Christ, this will turn out for my deliverance. It is my eager expectation and hope that I will not be put to shame in any way, but that by my speaking with all boldness, Christ will be exalted now as always in my body, whether by life or by death. For to me, living is Christ and dying is gain (1:19-21).

He wrote, "I don't know what I'm going to do," but in verse 24 he said, "But it is more necessary for you that I remain in the body." God's "Yes" to Paul, by definition, involved others. Paul, imprisoned, alone, and isolated from his friends at Philippi, could nevertheless celebrate God's "Yes" in community with others. For us to say, "God answered my prayer," and then go about our own self-centered business gives witness not to a mighty God, but to a shallow faith, a bankrupt theology, and worst of all, a selfish soul. For any of us to say, "God said 'Yes', " and then go do our own thing causes thinking Christians to ask, "Was the 'Yes' from God, or did I miss it?" God's "Yes" is no private blessing. Just as the faithful community is one source of hearing God's voice, so the community is also one recipient of God's blessings. Don't keep God's "Yes" to yourself. Share it with others.

There is one more thing—the most difficult of all. God's "Yes" is full of *risk*. We would be deceiving ourselves if we thought for one moment God's "Yes" is an end itself. Not so. Rather, God's "Yes" is a beginning, a passageway, a door to the next stage of life's journey. And entering that door, receiving God's "Yes" as our own, brings with it great risk.

As difficult as it is to hear and accept God's "No," hearing and accepting God's "Yes" may be the more difficult and dangerous answer God gives us. Why? Because when God says, "Yes," God places in our hands the heavy burden of an answered prayer and the provocative possibility of a new life as yet not considered.

"I've completed my education." Wonderful! Now what? "My cancer has been cured." Thanks be to God! Now what? We miss it if we think God's "Yes" is the end of something. No! God's "Yes" is always the beginning of a fuller and more empowered life: a life characterized by greater service, greater responsibility, greater accountability. God's "Yes" is not an end but a beginning. When you and I say, "God said 'Yes'," everything within us responds with "Wonderful," or "Thank the Lord." Now what will you say? Now what will you do? Now what will you become?

What will you say to God's "Yes?" How about, "Thank you"? Remember the parable Jesus told about the ten lepers? All were healed. Nine went away; one came back. We teach it to our children. That parable says many things, not the least of which is, 90 percent of us don't know how to say "Thank you." How about a prayer of gratitude? "Thank you, Lord." If "Thank you" were on our lips in prayer, scowls would be on our faces less, and smiles would be on our faces more. How about simply saying, "Thank you"?

There is great risk in God's "Yes." "Yes" is not an end but a beginning. What will you do? How about choosing to live affirmatively? How about putting down a positive stake in life and saying, "I will live for God," "I will live for others," "I will live for . . ."—you complete the sentence?

What will you become? Perhaps you would become God's "Yes" incarnate, becoming the "Yes" God has given you. God healed you? Yes! Who do you know who needs healing? Interact with them; pray for them; affirm them. They will draw strength from your "Yes," and, in sharing yourself, you will find God multiplying that one answered prayer in the lives of others.

God gave you a good job and a promotion. Yes! Who are those who still struggle for such benefits? Perhaps by investing your life in helping those who are not on life's fast track to just get on *a* track, you would become the "Yes" God has spoken to you. I tell you there is great risk in hearing a "Yes" from God—maybe more burdensome than God's "No"—because God's "Yes" is not an end but a beginning.

It dawned on me one day that the Bible in all of its glory is speaking God's "Yes" from beginning to end. The Living Word, thrown up on the stage of life, has line after line where we find God's "Yes." Believe it or not, I almost missed this empowering reality. Remember with me the last chapters of the book of Revelation. John the Seer had glimpsed all of the horror and confusion of a world in opposition to God. Then, in the final act of Revelation's drama, with inspired genius, John said, "Then I saw a new heaven and a new earth; for the first heaven and the first earth had passed away, and the sea was no more." (21:1). Having read that verse many times, it hit me that this is at the very core of the Bible's message. That all endings are beginnings, that all lasting answers lead to other questions and more affirmation, that all gifts summon us to even more extravagant giving, that even life itself, ending in death as it does, moves on to eternity, where both ending and beginning find their ultimate fulfillment in the One who is "the Alpha and the Omega, the beginning and the end."

So you say, "God has said 'Yes' to my prayers." Wonderful. I know you are grateful. I share your joy. Now what? At the end of our lives, when we drop this robe of flesh and rise in risen glory through the power of Jesus Christ, I suspect all of us in our own words and way will rise into his arms with "Yes" on our lips. And when the Savior meets us on that other shore, I imagine he will say, "This 'Yes' is only the beginning of life eternal; life you cannot imagine, that you cannot comprehend, but that you will live into with great joy in my presence."

So God said "Yes." Now what?

Father, help me to learn from those who have gone before me and from those who are going with me that you often answer my prayers in surprising, unexpected ways. Forgive me when I become so specific in prayer that I marginalize or, worse, eliminate any possibility of seeing an answer I had not anticipated. Remind me that I live in the midst of your glorious creation that is moving not toward an end but toward a beginning; that even death itself is not a "No" but is your "Yes," your invitation to life eternal. Alpha and Omega, having received a wonderful "Yes" from your throne of mercy, free me to live a life of affirmation that will bring glory to you. Through Jesus Christ, your eternal "Yes," I pray, Amen.

Chapter 8

UNEXPECTED SILENCE

Someone very early in my living-near-the-beach life placed a conch shell in my hand and said, "Listen." You know what I heard, don't you? I heard the ocean, roaring its majesty on to a timeless beach. Or did I? Of course I didn't hear the ocean. What I heard was the sound of air roaring through the cavernous twists of the conch shell's interior. The sound was *like* the ocean, but not the ocean. Today I love to pick up a conch shell—when I can find one—and repeat that childhood experience of listening to the ocean. So far, every conch I've placed on my ear—whether in a gift shop in Ohio or at Panama City in Florida—gives me the experience of hearing the ocean.

Point? When you place a conch shell to your ear, you expect to hear the ocean. Right so far. But what would happen if I placed a conch shell to my ear and heard nothing? I'd first look at it and make sure I was really holding a conch shell. Second, I might even shake it to see if an intruder had ruined the God-created symmetry within its walls. Finally, if I still heard nothing, I'd wonder if perhaps I was going deaf.

Prayer point? When you pray, when you lay your soul before God, when you experience creation and read the Word and know love in the community of faith, you expect to hear God. You do, don't you? I do. But what happens when our heart is listening for God's voice and there is only silence? When God is silent, what do we do? What do we think? How do we go on when the only thing our heart hears is divine silence?

To answer that question I invite you to visit some folks I've known who've experienced the silence of God. They have their own story, but, perhaps in that space marked out by silence, their story reads much like yours. These fellow travelers placed the conch shell of prayer to their ear, desperate for God's voice, and heard nothing. Was it God's silence, their deafness, or something else?

Matt and Teri's life together started out with such promise. His whole being beamed with business optimism; she was a second-year medical student. To borrow some old words, "They had life by the tail in a downhill run." But something sinister and destructive started to happen in their relationship. It was one of those many "something's" that happens not once, but over time. Communication became difficult and then adversarial and finally combative. You know what I'm talking about, don't you? Something happened, and neither of them knew when it happened or how.

When life's "something's" show up, how do you cope? Far too few of us cope by facing the something head on. The rest of us—most of us—simply ignore it (professionals use the word "denial"). Still others deal with life's somethings like an inconvenient and unexpected guest. They invite the "something" in, serve it some ice tea, and quickly remember the fabricated and artificial life they were living before it showed up; a life to which they quickly return hoping the "something" will disappear. They escape, another form of denial. Some of us handle life's "something's" that way.

With Matt and Teri's, the something could not be ignored or abandoned. They tried that; God knows they tried. But the weeks lengthened into months and the months into three painful years. You see, their something was a potentially malicious marital malignancy. Where once the "I love you's" drowned them in emotion, now they were alone on two distant, deserted, and different shores. Physically and financially they were safe. In fact, like many others today, they lived deceptively "safe" behind superficial social masks that parroted "I'm fine" to friends who thought Matt and Teri were Ken and Barbie (at least that's who their well-worn masks said they were).

Yes, they were externally safe, but inside—both inside their skin and inside their marriage—they were alone, lonely, and silent. Where once their making of love was passionate and tender, now they grabbed the bed's iron frame as if it were prison bars from which no one escapes. Where once they longed for privacy, where handholding and nuzzling could be wrapped in ever-deepening eye contact, now they longed for groups and parties and any excuse to get away from each other so as to be lost in shallow crowds.

Both of them, in their aloneness, their separateness, their private hell, in great silence, cried out, "O God, why this? Why me? Why us? Why now? Why?" And heaven was silent, puzzlingly silent, terrifyingly silent.

We all know couples like Matt and Teri. There are many more who've known the silence of God in other circumstances. I'm thinking of believers I've known through the years who threw words toward God and heard an eternal, deafening "nothing" in return. Two—a husband and wife—whose daughter-in-law was brutally murdered at the midpoint of six months of other tragedies including the death of a parent, a serious automobile accident, and a career catastrophe. All of that happened in one six-month parenthesis of pain. They prayed, their family prayed, I prayed, the church prayed, we all prayed. And so far as any of us could tell, heaven was silent.

Others come to my mind and to yours. Persons we know who are held without mercy in the agony of a loved one's battle with Alzheimer's disease. Parents whose children have a drug dependency, and no one knows or can know, lest the masks come off and the truth be known. Young adults who still cover the bruises of a parent's abuse. Men and women with ethnic distinctions of color and accent and education who know the lash of discrimination. And yes, who can fathom the agony met in the fierce wake of a suicide; the pain, the questions, the emptiness, the "if only's"? All of these and many more prayed to God with great faith and uncommon courage. They looked up, cried out, cast their very souls on God, and heard nothing. Heaven was silent.

Still there are more. Writing these lines between Mother's Day and Father's Day, I'm made aware—moreso with every passing year of ministry and life—of the many men and women who would give everything they have and will ever have for the blessing of being parents. They long with empty arms to bring a child into being and cannot. I can't help seeing their faces as I write these lines: husbands and wives who want to be parents but, for reasons known and unknown, cannot. Conception seems like a dream, adoption impossibly far away. Theirs is a pain I have not known. But through their pain, they have held on in faith through a silent season of life. They pray, they long, they hurt, they ask, and heaven is silent and God seems far off. There is only silence to hold them in their lingering, longing pain.

We who know life's pain know the silence of which I speak. Even those who for some reason have been spared such agony will, sooner or later, know this silence. You have known it, or will know it, in your own way. You've experienced it, or will experience it at some moment in life's journey—the silence of God. How is coping possible when even the lover of our souls says nothing and we hear nothing and there is only nothing? What do we do, and how can we go on?

Groping Through It

Many are the ways we handle God's silence. Some ways are helpful, others harmful. Some of our coping is mere groping; trying to feel our way through what for us is uncharted and dangerous territory. With honesty, I confess I have groped through my share of heaven's silences. Coping by groping makes sense at first, but such sense quickly gives way to further emptiness and greater silence.

More often than not, *words* seem to be an escape from silence. We assume that our much talking, our many prayers, our witty words can bury our pain beneath vowels, consonants, syllables, phrases, and clichés. Somehow we have bought into the idea that if we can just keep talking, we can talk our way out of the silence. But we know it doesn't work. Talk as we do and will, silence is still our companion, and God does not speak.

Like words, activity has a way of side-stepping heaven's silence. We go back to work, throw ourselves into something important, pick up a shovel and dig in the yard, take a golf club and hit a dozen balls into the sky . . . any activity—just something to make the silence seem not so silent. But alas, we cannot busy ourselves into hearing God who seems unprepared or unwilling to talk to us.

If groping words and frenetic activity will not shatter the silence, what will? All of us can probably identify with Brennan Manning's simple but profound sentence: "The experience of absence does not mean the absence of experience."[1] We have known and still know the experience of absence, and it has been so often a painful experience. Paul S. Fiddes, in his provocative book *The Creative Suffering of God*, distinguishes between God's absence and God's hiddenness. God, though silent, is not absent; God suffers with us and is there for us.[2] Could God's silence not mean God's absence? Perhaps God's silence is God's way of magnifying God's presence, silent though it may be.

Such was the witness of one in the long ago who plumbed the silences of God. Psalm 13 is populated with many words, but around, between, over, and above each one of them is great silence, but not absence. Listen to the witness of one who knew the silence of God.

> How long, O Lord? Will you forget me forever? How long will you hide your face from me? How long must I bear pain in my soul, and have sorrow in my heart all day long? How long shall my enemy be exalted over me?
>
> Consider and answer me, O Lord my God! Give light to my eyes, or I will sleep the sleep of death, and my enemy will say, "I have prevailed"; my foes will rejoice because I am shaken. But I trusted in your steadfast love; my heart shall rejoice in your salvation. I will sing to the Lord, because he has dealt bountifully with me.

What are we to make of this? What in and around and under the silence molded this faithful one into greater trust? As he always does, Frederick Buechner offers some help. He wrote nearly thirty years ago:

> Part of the inner world of everyone is this sense of emptiness, disease, incompleteness, and I believe that this in itself is a word from God, that this is the sound that God's voice makes in a world that has explained him away. In such a world I suspect that maybe God speaks to us most clearly through his silence, his absence, so that we know him best through our missing him.[3]

Could it be that our words and/or our activity–pious or profane–will never break God's silence? Buechner is on to something here. Could it be that the silence of God in no way diminishes God's presence? That our missing God—Manning's "experience of absence"—is a verification of the fact, the reality, that God is with us, perhaps in powerful ways, loving ways, tender ways? Could that be so?

We know it's so in other relationships. How many times have you simply slid your hand into your lover's and, with a gentle squeeze, pictured the bond that can never be broken? No words, simply presence. How many times have you found great strength emanating from a friend sitting across from you in a Sunday School classroom? You didn't speak; you didn't need to speak. Presence was enough. Could that be so with God? Could the silence of God actually be communicating to us in profound and loving ways God's steadfast presence?

Yet we seem unsatisfied and spiritually lost unless we have words, sound, noise, something. To our loss, and too often our greater pain, we live through the silence of God weighed down with words only to find ourselves on the other side of it embittered, angry, critical, and more lonely than ever before. Our words—angry words, caustic words, incriminating words—fill up the silence. Our words both accuse and explain. "If God were more loving, God would . . ." Or, "How could a God of love allow . . . ?"

From accusing and interrogating God, we can move to fault finding and analysis. Through it all we keep talking, filling up the silence with *our* words and *our* anger and *our* disappointment and *our* grief until *our* words are as knives severing the tender and loving cords that would wrap us in God's love. We really believe we can talk or busy the silence away, don't we?

Another Way

There is another way to handle the silences of God. The Psalmist—the silence-coping Psalmist we meet in Psalm 13—gives us some help. He tells us we can deal with the silences of God. Let's listen to the witness of one who did.

I heard the Psalmist say, "Ask God your questions." Put your questions to God, and wait for God's response. Four times in two verses the Psalmist asked God, "How long?" He put his question to God. Read it out loud. It's an "in your face" question, isn't it? His witness tells us we, too, can ask God our questions. But what do we do instead? So often we don't voice our questions to God. We voice our questions to people.

We ask others struggling with the same questions, "Where is God?" "How could a God of love allow this to happen." We question God's presence and even God's integrity by asking others the questions we need to ask God. We ask questions alright, not to God, but to others. Such questioning is doomed to failure.

Lest we be too critical of ourselves, we tend to do the very same thing in our relationships with others. If we're having a problem in our relationship with a friend, rather than going to her and saying, "I have a concern. I'm hurting. We need to talk," what do we do? We go out and talk to other people about her and our problems with her. Doing so only deepens the hurt, widens the gap between us, and raises the almost certain possibility we will never resolve the crisis. This is sheer relational lunacy. It's un-Christian and an arrogant disregard for the teaching of Jesus in Matthew 18:15-17.

The Psalmist offers us another way. Are we listening? When God is silent, throw your questions up to God. Ask God the "How long?" questions. In asking God, at least you will be directing your concerns to the appropriate person. How long? In the midst of experiencing God's silence, it's okay to question God. Job did, Paul did, David did, Jesus did, and throughout the history of humanity, faithful people have questioned God. You'll not be the first nor the last.

The Psalmist continued. Having voiced our questions to God, we can know that God is there, was there, and will be there for us. "Look on me and answer, O Lord my God" (v. 3) is a demand put to God who is there. When God is silent we can so quickly suspect, imagine, conjecture, that God has gone. God has disappeared; if not completely, at least God has disappeared for me.

The Psalmist offers us another way. The Psalmist speaks of God's presence in relationship. We can question God, believing God is eternally with us. This is the promise of God in Christ. Just as Gabriel told Joseph Jesus would be "Immanuel," meaning "God with us" (Matt 1:23), so God is with us now. The One who came incarnate in flesh is the very One among us now as Holy Spirit. The Promised One is the Present One; Jesus said the Comforter would be "with you and will be in you" (John 14:17). There is relationship in the here-ness of God. God is present. We can address God personally. Through Christ, God is ever with us and in us by God's Spirit.

As I noted earlier, some of life's most intimate experiences are enjoyed in silence, a silence shared with persons for whom we deeply care who embrace us and love us and are there for us. In their presence we don't say a word. We don't have to. But we know they are there. In the silence, remember, God is with you. Epictetus, though a non-Christian philosopher, nevertheless spoke the truth when he said, "When thou hast shut thy door and darkened thy room, say not to thyself that thou art alone. God is in thy room."[4]

Believers who meditate know the power of silence. Rather than being driven into silence by horrific and painful circumstances, many believers search out the silence and find great strength. The discipline of Christian meditation has an empowering, focusing quality about it that can center life in the presence of God. Thrust into silence, however, we move toward disciplined meditation by simply being with God and letting God's silence nurture us and love us back into spiritual health. Working through the silence in our pain can nudge us toward silence as a way of growing spiritually in our relationship with God.

There is one last thought. In the silences of God (between pain and promise, questions and answers), when heaven is hushed, the Psalmist reminds us to *trust*. In verse 5, after the Psalmist has gone through a litany of words giving witness to the silence of God, we read, "But I trust . . . ."

Here is a significant milemarker on life's faith journey. When all we think is important comes crashing down around us and we throw our words up to God and question the awesome, awfulness of it all, can we come to the place where we say, "But I trust" and go on? Because if trust is not in the picture, if trust is not there in our relationship with God, we've got a larger problem than God's silence. Is it not so that even to voice the word "God" is to incarnate the word trust. With confidence, surrounded by silence, we can believe in our being that God is there and, with greater courage, say, "But I trust."

Jesus knew this trust spoken of in the Psalms. On that night of nights in an upper room in old Jerusalem, a night when words would be spoken and a meal shared, a friend abandoned and a trial convened, Jesus plumbed the eternal depths of silence. In that moment, as a cross was being hewn out of fear and nails were being struck on the anvil of madness, when the deafening silence of heaven would be as starkly silent as it would ever be, Jesus said, "Come away. Come to this table. Break this bread. Share this cup. In a little while, we are going to a garden where the silence will be greater. And yes, I'm going to a cross where silence will be my only companion." In those upper room-olive garden-kangaroo court-bloody cross moments, suspended as they were between the roaring "Hosanna's" of Sunday and the jeering "Crucify's" of Friday, Jesus was dropped into a silence known only in hell. Somehow, by the mercy of God, he endured it all, held by a trust that went with him to his death. He trusted until he breathed his last breath.

And what of this crucified and bloody trust the mob called "stupid" and the disciples never understood? The record tells us that on the other side of Friday's silence, endured only with trust, was and still is an Easter glory. That is the Good News Christians celebrate and into which Christians live. The trust that sustained Jesus in death is the trust that can sustain you in life and in death and always.

So heaven is silent, is it? God is saying nothing. Be still. No, better yet, be quiet; shut up, and listen. For even in the silence where there are no words, answers, reasons, explanations, theories, clichés—no anything—there is the Christ who knows the silence through which you are living. He has been there and even now is there with you. That alone is reason to trust.

God of all creation, you shattered the silence of eternity past with your creative and creating Word. In Jesus Christ, Word became flesh, and that flesh spoke and laughed and sang and cried. His was an audible Presence, shattering the noisy silence of our confused world. And yet, I am here hungry for your Word, hearing nothing. O Living Christ, when your voice is silent and your silence voiced, assure me by your presence I am not alone. In the silence, in the nothing that is your Word's absence, be to me your certain presence. Through Immanuel, even Christ, I pray, Amen.

Notes

[1]Brennan Manning, *The Ragamuffin Gospel* (Sisters OR: Multnomah Books, 1990) 82.

[2]Paul S. Fiddes, *The Creative Suffering of God* (Oxford: Clarendon Press, 1988) 191-92.

[3]Frederick Buechner, *The Magnificent Defeat* (New York: Seabury, 1966) 47-49.

[4]Quoted by Harry Emerson Fosdick in *The Meaning of Prayer*, in *Voices from the Heart: Four Centuries of American Piety* (Grand Rapids: Wm. B. Eerdmans Publishing Co., 1987) 262.

Chapter 9
LATER, EVENTUALLY, SOMETIME

Can you remember being nine years old? It was early April. Winter was a cold memory, and spring was in the air. You knew summer was just around the corner. As you walked down Main Street in the town where you lived, or strolled through the mall with your Mom or Dad, you kept looking for the store window with the bicycles in it. You didn't care about trying on summer clothes or the fact Mom had to return a shirt she'd bought for your Dad he didn't like. No. You had one thing on your shopping list: getting to the store with the bicycles so you could put the full court press on your mother to buy one for you.

Carefully, you'd written your speech a hundred times in your mind. You *needed* it. All your friends had a new bike except you. Buying the bike would prove your parent's love for you. All the lines were carefully rehearsed. Finally, you rounded the corner, Mom in tow, and there it was: bright red, shiny spokes, ten speeds, hand brakes, the works. You were nine; the bicycle was brand new.

At that point, the cost of the bicycle was light-years from your mind. You didn't know about money, a family budget, or a mortgage. You knew one thing. You had to have that bicycle. It was spring, summer was coming, and you had a lot of bike riding to do with your friends. Your parents knew (didn't they?) that your old bike was a little rusty, the chain was a little rough, the tires were lumpy, and the seat was worn out. You knew it, and you couldn't face another summer creaking along with your friends in your jalopy of a bike.

But right there, in front of that store, your future—as bright as the paint on the ten speed—was staring you in the face. You knew you had to have that bicycle. So, speech ready, emotion welling up in your throat, you looked up into the face of your Mom and said, "Could I have that bicycle?" And she looked down into your eyes and said, "We'll think about it." Instantly, all the air went out of your tires. You knew your parents. You'd lived with them nine years, hadn't you? "We'll think about it" usually meant "No." It doesn't take a child very long to figure it out.

Of course, they may have said, "Why don't you ask Santa Claus?" Or, "Sooner or later" (and that always meant later). Psychologists call this "delayed gratification," and not a one of us likes it. You don't have to be nine. You could be ninety. None of us likes delayed gratification. I don't like it; you don't like it; we don't like it.

So it is in our relationship with God. As the listening heart tunes itself to hear the voice of God, the one answer we don't quite know how to handle is "Later." What do you do when you lay your very soul before God, offer your petitions before God's throne of grace, and the answer you receive is either "Later," "Not now," "Eventually," or "Sometime"? I don't know about you, but instinctively, I'll plead, bargain, and often argue with God. I'm especially fond of giving God additional information in the hope of convincing God of my need for a more immediate, affirmative answer to my prayer. God is not impressed. The answer is "Later," and I'm not happy about it.

Why? Because our experience with parents as children and with others as adults has convinced us "Later" means "Never." Is that so? The opposite may be true; "Never" could turn out to mean "Later." I'm thinking of some people who, in recent human history, were told either "No" or "Never," and yet they heard "Later." The President of South Africa, Nelson Mandela, was told "Never" for twenty-seven years as the prisoner of the white-led South African government. The government said to Mandela and all minorities in that country, "Never." But Mandela and all those of color heard God say, "Later."

I'm thinking about African-Americans who for hundreds of years were told "Never." But they heard God say, "Later." In the midst of the Civil War, Abraham Lincoln signed the Emancipation Proclamation. One hundred years later President Lyndon Johnson signed the Voting Rights Act. Today we are still in the process of moving through the experience of making sure as a society that all people have equal justice and equal rights under law. There was a time when African-Americans were told "Never." Yet they heard God say, "Later." "Later" may not be God's most confusing answer, but it surely gives us our share of difficulty.

Go to the Bible. Meet a people who heard year after year, century after century God's "later." It's risky, but let's collapse two thousand years of history into just a handful of sentences. God called Abraham to be the father of a great nation. He took Israel's patriarch out in the middle of a dark, Middle Eastern night and said, "Look up old man, and count the stars. Look down, count the sands of the sea. So shall your descendants be." Then late in life God gave Abraham and Sarah the gift of Isaac and to Isaac and Rebekah, God gave Esau and Jacob, the younger Jacob receiving the blessing. The centuries passed, and the family became a people. There was an exile in Egypt and a glorious deliverance.

Nations fell, the delivered people came together, and for one brief shining moment there was a kingdom over which David ruled and later, his son Solomon. But the military exploits of David and the genius of Solomon were all short-lived. Following Solomon's death, the kingdom split in two. First the Assyrians conquered the northern kingdom of Israel, and then the Babylonians came and subdued the southern kingdom of Judah. The people were carted off into exile, all the time longing, praying for the kingdom to be restored, for their place in the sun. And through the pain and humiliation, through the centuries, those who prayed kept hearing "Later."

Finally, Jesus of Nazareth walked on to the stage of history. He spoke of a Kingdom that was near, that was coming, that was even in the midst of us all. He said, "The Kingdom of God is within you." But too soon, the sons and daughters of Adam and Eve strung him up. When the likes of you and I got our hands on him, we nailed him to the cross, dusted off our hands, and said, "That's all for him." And still the Kingdom had not come.

Later, on the third day, God visited Jesus' grave in resurrection power; Christ the Lord rose in glory. He assembled those who had forsaken him and, to their starry-eyed amazement, brought them into his confidence again. Listen and witness the last conversation Jesus had with his disciples as recorded by Dr. Luke in the book of Acts.

> While staying with them, he ordered them not to leave Jerusalem, but to wait there for the promise of the Father. "This," he said, "is what you have heard from me; for John baptized with water, but you will be baptized with the Holy Spirit not many days from now."
>
> So when they had come together, they asked him, "Lord, is this the time when you will restore the kingdom to Israel?" He replied, "It is not for you to know the times or periods that the Father has set by his own authority. But you will receive power when the Holy Spirit has come upon you, and you will be my witnesses in Jerusalem, in all Judea and Samaria, and to the ends of the earth." (1:4-8).

A kingdom? Israel? "What about now, Lord?" Jesus said, "Later." Could we learn how to handle God's "later" to us from Jesus' response to the disciples? I think so.

Jesus is saying some very specific truths about how to handle prayer's postponed answers. First, I heard the risen Lord speak four powerful words: "Wait for the promise." "Wait," though not an imperative in the Greek, has the force of an imperative. In the strongest of words, the strongest words the Greek language could use, Jesus said to the disciples, "*Do not* leave Jerusalem, *but wait* for the promise of the Father" (emphasis mine).

When God says, "Later," why don't we try waiting for the gift God promises? We all know, don't we, how hard it is to wait for the gift because, if the truth were known, all of us would rather have an answer than a gift. We pray, we beg, we ask, we long. I suppose we don't put it in words like this to God, but our response gives us away. "God, if you could just put the answer on a 3x5 index card. You can write in long hand if you want; I can read your writing. Give me the answer."

God, whom we meet in Jesus Christ, is obviously short on answers and apparently long on gifts. Yet we act as if we'd rather have an answer than a gift. But the gospel, born of sacrifice and given as grace, knows only of gifts given to spiritually impoverished folks like us. How ironic it is that in this present "Information Age," an era of human history in which we are literally drowning in data, we lust for more data, blinded to the gifts God generously wants to give us. Like Peter and the rest of the disciples, we'd rather control a kingdom of information—that means power—than serve the risen Christ. "Restore the kingdom to Israel" means, "Give us the power." Our Lord's response to the disciples was clear. "You can't handle that, but you can receive a gift born of Holy Spirit power. You have a job to do. Wait for the gift."

We humans do not like to hear "later," "wait," "sometime," "eventually," and "not now." Delayed gratification is something none of us like, but it's so much a part of life, isn't it? I feel compelled to name a great duplicity loose in our society swirling around this thing called delayed gratification. I've been racking my brain for a long time trying to find a handle for it. On the one hand, most of us post-World War II people receive mail, almost weekly, containing applications for credit cards. At our place, we sometimes get one or two a week. Of course the "come-on" letter says "low interest rate," "high credit line," and "no annual fee" (except, of course for the 21% interest you'll pay on your unpaid balance). All of us—individually and collectively—are being consumed by this "buy now, pay later" mentality. Delayed gratification? Hardly!

Studies tell us that, in many cases, credit card debt is the number-one monster crippling families. Why? You know why. When we're asked, "How would you like to pay for that?" we say, "Charge it." Our parents and grandparents know better. They pay cash. But we baby boomers and busters have bought the idea: if you want it now, buy it now, and pay for it later.

And what of the duplicity I sense lurking in the shadows? The duplicity—pundits call it "doublespeak"—rears its ugly head when the very people who are charging now and paying and paying and paying later tell their teenagers, "Save sex for marriage. Save intimate, physical relationships for the person with whom you'll spend the rest of your life. That's one 'later' worth waiting for." That's what we say, but what we live is: "Buy now, pay later at the department store, but wait—in the midst of irrational passion—for sexual intimacy until marriage." Our young people are not waiting because one of the big messages we are sending to them as a society is, "Nobody waits for anything." And in not waiting, both young and old seize an answer, gratify an urge, satisfy a hunger now, and loose the gift wrapped up for later. Other examples abound. We've lived them and are living them.

Jesus said, "Wait for the gift." In our haste, we rush headlong before God's throne of grace and mercy, begging and pleading with God only to hear "Later." And then what? We go out on our own and wrest answers for ourselves. We may get what we want *our* way, but in doing so, we miss the gift that awaits us in God's "later" moment. Wait for the gift.

One of the more difficult lessons God has taught me as a pastor has to do with this "now" and "later" standoff. Anyone who knows me knows I am a "hands-on" person. I enjoy being with the people who call me "Pastor," sharing their lives and praying they will "take me in" as both minister and person. God's "later" has often blessed me in the lives of people who stood at a distance from me for years, afraid to approach me, perhaps even "turned off" by what comes across as a threatening "in your face" way of relating to people. The "later" gift cannot be manufactured; only God can give it. Try as I have and still do to encourage people to let me into their lives, that only comes as a gift and normally comes "later." The listening heart knows that God's gift comes wrapped in patient trust born of a faith in God whose "later" may be God's best. Where is God inviting you to wait for the gift?

Jesus hinted at something else that day outside Jerusalem. Namely, *listen carefully to your prayers*. The listening heart not only tunes itself to God's voice, but must ever be listening to its own sound. Do you remember the first time you heard your own voice on audiotape? Frightening, wasn't it? "I don't sound like *that*, do I?" The tape doesn't lie. Yep! That's you. All of us would be helped immeasurably if we'd take time—and often—to "tape" our prayers and listen. Perhaps shock would give way to learning and learning to maturity. All of us can grow by listening to our own prayers.

Look again at the risen Lord's conversation with the disciples in Acts 1:4-6. Focus on those three verses. I've read them dozens and dozens of times. I've read them in the Greek and multiple English translations. I've even preached on this text before and never noticed a startling fact until recently. Look at verses 4 and 5. Verse 4 begins, "While he was staying with them, he ordered them not to leave Jerusalem, but to wait." After he gave them these instructions, he left them. In verse 6, a second meeting is recorded. That verse begins, "So when they had come together." Do you see it? Jesus gathered the disciples together first and said, "Don't leave Jerusalem. Wait for the gift." And then he left. Some time elapsed, and then he appeared to them again, as recorded in verse 6.

I've read that passage many times and assumed Acts 1:4-6 recorded one meeting between the risen Lord and the disciples. Not so. Two meetings. When this hit me, I began thinking about the conversation Peter, Andrew, James, and John—the four leaders of the disciple band—had after Jesus told them they were to wait for the gift. Can you see those guys? Use your imagination. Here's what may have happened.

Jesus says, "Wait for the gift." He leaves. As soon as he disappears, Peter calls the disciples together. "Here he goes again. For three years we followed him around Galilee and Judea, and he kept saying, 'The Kingdom of God is near.' He kept talking about the lilies of the field and the birds of the air and a Kingdom that was breaking into our world. Look where it got us. He talked about gifts for years. He talked about God taking care of us. Look where it got us. This 'Kingdom talk' put him on a cross and, if we are not careful, we'll be next."

So, being the forerunners of all church leaders who would follow them, they called a committee meeting. They brought the committee together and decided how they would respond to Jesus the next time he appeared to them. Peter, of course, did the talking. One of the others wrote down the words. "How will we phrase the question to him when he comes back?" This conversation surely went into the wee hours of the next morning.

Sure enough, Jesus returned for another meeting with the disciples. Notice how verse 6 is worded: "So when they had come together, *they* asked him." They didn't all speak in unison, but it was their question; every one of them had a stake in this. "Lord, we've met and decided this 'wait for the gift' promise is not really what we need. What we need is a kingdom now. So, seeing as we've met and sorted it all out, would you at this time restore the kingdom to Israel?" Laugh if you want, but that's the sense of these verses nestled in and around every word.

"Later? We've got a better idea."

Are we listening to our prayers? This one verse—Acts 1:6—summarizes so many of our prayers. "Lord, will you do this for me?" "Lord, will you answer my prayer, this prayer, for me, right now?" This is a model of petitionary prayer turned in on itself. We address God as Sovereign Lord and then start giving God our list of demands. No quicker than you can scratch a comma, the disciples pulled out their wish list, and the first item on the list was, "Will you restore the kingdom to Israel?"

What's on your list? I reviewed my list recently and discovered to my shame (and perhaps you would discover to yours) that my list was full of me, mine, and ours. My health, my job, our security, my wants, our needs, me, us, our, I. What's on your list?

Are we listening to our prayers? Turn the tape recorder on and listen. Here's an assignment. It's a prayer assignment and a difficult one. This week—for one brief week: seven days—why not take yourself out of your prayers? Why not spend ten minutes each day this week in prayer for the moms and dads, boys and girls of the war-torn quarters of our world, where children are dying in the clutches of war? What we want might not seem so important.

What about spending ten minutes a day praying for AIDS babies; little boys and girls born into a terror not of their choosing? Perhaps if we did that, our wish list, our demands, our wants might not seem so important. Why not spend ten minutes in prayer for the homeless and in all of those minutes refuse to talk about yourself? If you find those assignments difficult, try spending ten minutes praising God. Taking your eyes off self and focusing them on God is a powerful way of putting all of life under the sovereignty of God. As difficult as it is, try removing "me" from your prayers.

Our world, so broken by the selfishness of governments, individuals, and yes, even religion, is withering under the unforgiving heat of a demanding humanity. God's "later" is one way God is saying to us, "I have more urgent crises around the world—the world for which my Son died and rose again—than answering your personal, selfish, controlling, and often manipulative prayers." "Later" is God's way of telling us God's "something else" is breaking into our "now." That "something else" may be personal. My hunch is, based upon the prayers God answered with "later" from Scripture, God's "something else" is much larger, much more comprehensive than our personal wish list. Something greater is coming into our now, if we would but see it. "Later" is God's way of saying, "I need you to participate in the work I am doing now." Can you hear God saying, "What you need is a 'later' matter compared to the task of bringing this world into the love of Christ"?

There also is a personal dimension to it all. We may be so hung up on wanting what we want now, and angry because God has said "later," that we miss all the joy and power of living between "now" and "later." Some hospital visits are etched deeply in my mind. I walked into his hospital room, and after a few greetings he said something to me I'll never forget. He had been diagnosed with cancer and had gone through the first of many treatments. He was angry and confused, as you or I would be. He looked into my eyes and said, "I almost missed it." I said, "You almost missed what?" He said, "I almost missed it. My granddaughter . . . my eleven-year-old granddaughter stood at my bedside this week and said to me, 'Grand-daddy, I'm so glad you are alive.' "

The tears were beginning to well up in his eyes. I wasn't sure he would be able to continue. Wiping his cheeks with the sleeve of his hospital gown, he went on. "I was so caught up in my anger and my bitterness, demanding from God that I be healed, I almost missed the 'I love you's' coming from the people I love most. I almost missed it." In those moments, between that "now" and some distant "later," God spoke, and both the patient and I were held in the embrace of the awesome and loving voice that is God's.

When you stop and think about it a few minutes, we are all going to die from something. There are some among us who have named the something. We think we know what the diagnosis is and how the disease will progress and how the ultimate end will come. Some among us think we know the "something." Believe it or not, all of us have a something. And if we are not careful, we'll get so wrapped up in dealing with the "something," we'll miss experiencing this precious gift of life, with all its "I love you's" dancing around our ten square miles of reality. He said, "I almost missed it." Listen carefully to your prayers. Sometimes God says, "Later."

There is one more gift Jesus would have us hear. I think I heard him say, "Live toward a greater promise." When the disciples and the risen Lord gathered outside Jerusalem, he answered their request for a Kingdom, just not in the way they wanted. Do you remember what he said? "It is not for you to know the times or periods that the Father has set by his own authority. But you will receive power when the Holy Spirit has come upon you, and you will be my witnesses." Meaning? There is a Kingdom, but it is a Kingdom whose borders are bold witness and daring ministry and sacrificial living and amazing grace. Meaning? God's "Later" is a future none of us ever completely comprehend. We live within the borders of the Kingdom—within its power and its grace—knowing full well the Kingdom is not ours, but God's. Understood in these terms, the entire Christian movement is a "later" phenomenon.

For example, when I was fifteen years of age, Dr. Ernest R. Campbell baptized me "in the name of the Father, and the Son, and the Holy Spirit." As I was going under those waters, he quoted Paul's confession in Romans 6: "We are buried with Christ in baptism, raised to walk in newness of life." From that moment until now I've been trying to understand and live into the meaning of those words. The only way I can understand them at all is to accept the fact my baptism was a prelude to God's "later" when, redeemed by God's love and saved by God's grace, I stand in God's presence freed from both the penalty and power of sin. Baptism is one witness to God's promise that "later" will come.

So "Later" is not "No" or "Never" or "Sometime." Rather, "Later" is the great promise that God is not finished with any of us or any of "it" as yet. There is more. When the early Christians remembered the life and teachings of our Lord, thank God the Holy Spirit reminded them of the Model Prayer. Remember the line in the prayer that says, "Thy kingdom come, thy will be done on earth as it is in heaven."

Thinking about those words has driven me to see it was just like Peter, Andrew, James, and John to remember that prayer. As long as they lived, as long as they preached, as long as they served, they kept praying, "Thy kingdom come, thy will be done on earth as it is in heaven." They kept praying and living for the Kingdom to come on earth, but they didn't go to their upper room and bolt the door and shut the world out. Rather, they entered the world empowered with the Holy Spirit's power and lived and preached and died conscious of God's "later," knowing their responsibility in the "now."

Could we do the same? When God says "Later," when God says "Not now," when God says "Sometime" to our prayers, could we rise, remember, and celebrate God's promise breaking into our lives even now? In the larger picture of reality framed by the gospel, the most enduring, meaningful wonders of faith cannot be realized until later.

I learned a gospel song as a child you may know as well. I don't know how I learned it, but these lines are scribbled with indelible ink on my mind.

> O they tell me of a home far beyond the skies,
> O they tell me of a home far away;
> O they tell me of a home where no storm clouds rise,
> O they tell me of an unclouded day.
>
> O the land of cloudless day,
> O the land of an unclouded day;
> O they tell me of a home where no storm clouds rise,
> O they tell me of an unclouded day.

The song—every line of it—is saying and singing "Later." So my friend, when you tune your heart to God's voice, listening for some word from the One who created you and loves you, don't be surprised if you hear "Later." Remember, "O they tell me of a home far, far, far beyond the skies, O they tell me of a later, eventually, sometime, certain unclouded day."

Father, help me to live in the now fully aware of your later. Through your Word and the witness of your people, remind me that all of your promises have been tied with beautiful resurrection ribbon in Jesus Christ. By your Spirit, give me a listening heart to understand that my present difficulty and confusion, my unanswered, postponed prayer can be an opportunity for me to live with greater trust and greater hope. Save me from missing the "I love you's" of life, and free me to live toward that day when the clouds are no more. In Jesus' name, Amen.

Conclusion

PRAYER AND THE LISTENING HEART

And so our journey comes to an end. But perhaps not. Perhaps our time exploring prayer as listening eventuates in a pause, knowing such journeys begun only end in the presence of God where listening is transformed into worship and worship into God who is all in all.

Questions remain unanswered and perhaps beyond the scope of answering. The gift of a month's sabbatical freed me to complete this manuscript begun as five sermons. In dialogue with students and faculty at Oxford University's Regent's Park College, I have discovered a glaring but not unplanned omission. What about the heart's listening to God as an activity unto itself? Must world, Word, and community be involved in this empowering drama through which we hear God's voice? Can't we simply go to the closet, as Jesus advised, and shut out and turn off all external stimuli, and pray?

Of course we can—and we must. Omitting contemplative prayer, meditation, and solitude is not accidental. Quite the contrary. The candid truth is, none of us ever go to a prayer closet without taking a host of partners with us, including the world, the Word, and the community. Try as we may to hear God's voice in absolute, pure solitude and silence, we have with us companions who cannot be excused, avoided, or silenced.

Some of those noisy companions are guilt, sin, our humanity, and the devil. These compete with God's voice for our attention and often win hands down. To pray is to find oneself thrown into a noisy room where many voices clamor for attention, including God's. The listening heart, however, assaulted as it is by detractors of all kinds, longs for God and can discover in its quest faithful partners who speak of God's faithfulness. Three of those faithful companions are creation, Word, and the people of God.

Another question awaiting an answer has to do with the heart's relationship to the whole person. What part of me prays? The Bible seems to indicate, both in creation and salvation, that the listening heart and the person are inseparably bonded to one another in a psychosomatic union of spirit and flesh. What part of me prays? I pray, in the totality of my personhood. That personhood has been and continues to be shaped, blessed, and challenged by creation's order and chaos, the Word's clarity and ambiguity, and the faithful community's fidelity and sin. It is sheer lunacy to think any of us can pray, garrisoned in a closet, believing there we can truly hear God untouched by emotional, spiritual, physical, or emotional distractions. Such prayer may be possible in our dreams, but does not exist and cannot exist in reality.

Why? Because to pray listening for God's voice is to bring into our experience all God has done and is doing. God has created and is creating. God has spoken and is speaking. God has called humanity into community and calls us still. These gifts from God—world, Word, and people—become our heart's companions in our quest to hear and celebrate God's voice.

One question remains. Having heard and still hearing God's voice, what will we do? How will life be challenged and changed and blessed through the listening heart? That is the task awaiting us all as we live faithfully into the future God has for us.

In my judgment, the experience of prayer in these days is not about discovering more and better ways to commune with God. Rather, the issue is, having tuned our hearts to God's voice, what are we hearing, and how is our hearing affecting our living? My hunch is we are hearing more of God than we are applying in our lives. Personally, I know far more of God's voice and God's heart and God's love than I am prepared to share with others.

If that is so, the listening heart must become the giving heart. Only I can choose to give away the gifts God has given me. And you? What have you heard God say? What of God's voice is overflowing from your heart that others would receive as gift? Authentic prayer, heart communion with God, is no private blessing, is it? Jesus was right. When we pray, we are to say "*Our* Father," not "My

Father." Such prayer, by definition, brings others into the orbit of hearing God's voice through the human instrumentality of my life and your life and our lives.

So the journey continues. The listening heart can and must tune itself to hear the voice of God. Placed within creation, engaged with the Word, and participating in community, the listening heart, the prayerful person, longs for the sound of God's voice and, having heard the voice that spoke all that is into existence, finds itself being an expression of God's presence in this noisy world. For that reason, we who have heard cannot be silent.